All Poems written by Paul Colvin.

The cover for this book would never have been done if Garry Cross had not asked if I needed a hand with the artwork. The artist he had in mind was Nicole and a very special thanks goes out to her for the beautiful illustration of the Scottish Unicorn which I think is amazing. I am sure Nicole, you will be asked to do many more. I absolutely love it, thank you x.

I'd also like to give a special mention to Lisbeth Taylor for keeping me informed throughout and sending me The Common Weal book , THAT Sunday Herald paper, The National plus the stickers, pens and my YES Saltire. Thank you Lisbeth.

It really was an honour and a privilege being asked to write these poems for all you Yessers everywhere, and I hope you enjoy reading them.

Paul x

Foreword.

I write poetry as a pastime, usually on the bus going to and from work or relaxing at night when my mind is a bit freer. I have always been encouraged by Carmela Langella, my beautiful girlfriend, who believed I should be doing more to get my poetry read. She stood by me all the way, always believing.

I wrote a couple, on Scottish Independence, and posted them in facebook and the encouragement, comments and compliments received, gave me the confidence to open a page dedicated to Independence and brought about: https://www.facebook.com/PoemsforIndependence.

I have based these poems on truths, or to put it another way, what the media report so if they are lies, I can blame them. As most of my friends know, I had no vote in the referendum as I live in London, having moved from Glasgow in 1980 but Scotland and its people deserve to be free as do the rest of the UK from Westminster's greed.

These poems were written for the referendum and though that has come and gone, I think they are still relevant today.

The vote was NO but as I write Labour, for all their lies, has almost diminished in Scotland whilst the SNP has grown at an alarming rate, almost 93,000 Members, a new FM in Nicola Sturgeon after Alex Salmond stepped down, SSP and the Green Party have seen massive increases in their Memberships and long may that continue. The General Election will ultimately let the politicians know who the people believe. Roll on the 7th May 2015!

To

Margaret,

thank you for all your support & encouragement and hope you enjoy the book.

Paul x

Saor Alba gu Brath.

Introduction.

These poems were written for you in the lead up to the Scottish Referendum but I was asked to carry on writing afterwards. The disappointment was devastating but the people of Scotland refused to lie down after the lies of Westminster won with their No vote. They rose up, united, against the machine of Westminster with their marches and rallies and the bias of the "controlled media".

They showed their loyalty to the Labour Party by ripping up their Memberships and switching their allegiances to the SNP whose Membership increased by 300% in just two months and the SSP along with The Green Party also saw a significant rise. Labour, who bedded down with the coalition government throughout, have seen their Membership collapse and could actually lose 45 of their 50 seats at the next general election on 7th May 2015. How I hope that happens! The people of Scotland, and not only those who voted Yes, will never forget what they done. In the two months since the referendum, we have seen Darling, Brown and Lamont resign.

We have also seen one of Great Britain's greatest political leaders of recent times step down as First Minister of Scotland, Alex Salmond, only to be replaced by Nicola Sturgeon, his deputy. Westminster fear him and rightly so but he leaves in charge of the country he so nearly took to Independence, a very formidable leader in Ms Sturgeon. She took on a tour of Scotland where, on the first night in Glasgow, she spoke to a sell-out crowd of 12,000 whilst next door a further 3,000 attended a conference for The Radical Independence Party. Super star status for The Queen of Caledonia.

The Prime Minister of Great Britain, meanwhile, could only command a crowd of 100 and they were all handpicked!

Better Together cheated and lied their way to victory, terrifying senior citizens with the threat of losing their pensions if they voted Yes. This referendum was applauded worldwide because of the citizens' political involvement yet was constantly scandalised by the non-controlled media as to being the most distasteful ever because of the dirty tactics used by Better Together.

William MacRae.

In the highlands near Fort William, a car lies across a stream

A man lay slumped and dying but all's not as it seems

They thought it was a car crash or maybe suicide

But the evidence we looked for was quickly cast aside

Scotland had just lost William MacRae.

Two briefcases were yards away, beside them papers lay

And a gun was there beside them, belonging to, William MacRae

Not once but twice they shot him, two bullets to the brain

He frightened "them", he knew too much, about their nuclear waste campaign.

An SNP man murdered, who were "they"?

The Secret Service, MI5, it's their job to infiltrate

Did they know the route he took? Did they lie in wait?

One bullet yes to suicide but two, you must decide

His gun was just a pistol, from an automatic gun he died!

The police were forced to leave this unresolved.

*Before his death he'd tell his friends, "His cover" had been
blown*

*They didn't get what they were looking for but his life was
not his own*

*They'd plant their spies in meeting rooms, phones tapped of
every call*

The MI5 could find no flaws but their leader spoke for all

A radical, a lawyer, acting for the Free.

*Murrell, Peachman, many more, were killed fighting for
their cause*

*More were jailed for speaking out, in their Scotland that
once was*

*They spoke of Independence then; this freedom's nothing
new*

It's come full circle once again and is now long overdue.

Aye!

For You!

(This is for every one of you who have knocked on doors, set up stalls and worked so hard, unpaid, towards Scotland's independence. I thank you).

They set up stall, your vote to gain

In spite of weather or terrain

Their minds alert, their spirits high

Your options are, vote YES or AYE!

The tables set and stocked with fayre

In every town and village square

Countrywide, in cities too

You'll know them all, they look like you!

Painters, teachers, brickies, clerks,

From every walk, they'll leave their mark

An aptitude they hope to share,

With commitment way beyond compare.

They plot their way through every scheme

Canvassing their hopes and dreams

Against a regime out of touch

And London's slimy, greedy clutch

Though volunteers, their words enthuse

Because Scotland has too much to lose!

Unpaid, unnerved they take control

And boost the YES vote in the polls

The consequence of such a force

Will gain their wish, a sweet divorce.

Stick It!

Plaster yer windaes, wrap up your doors

Strap up yer wheelies make yer hoose yours

Put oan yer badges, take oot yer pen

And make yersel known through yer hills and yer glens

Don't listen tae Labour and the fear that they spread

Put up yer posters that's what they a' dread

Feart ae a Yes sign, too bloody true

These are yer neighbours, they'll listen tae you

They're frightened that Yes will take o'er No

That's jist us tellin' them where they can go

Democracy's callin' so dae whit you want

Tell them ye can, you don't understand can't!

Goodbye Westminster.

Look around at all you've lost then tally up that total cost

Did you receive your dividends or was that just for David's friends

These friends, already millionaires, are richer still through all their shares

Our gold was sold at half the price and The Royal mail was twice as nice

The greedy rubbed their hands with glee, less for them and more for me

And the NHS is next for sale and then your ground dug up for shale

They've kept the oil and kept their gall, they're racketeers and raped us all

They always think that they are right yet we look on without a fight

They played our hearts and preyed on minds and while we watched, they robbed us blind

As they coin it in, their pockets bulge but not a name will they divulge

They do not care nor do they heed, their only love is that of greed

Yet our politicians lay the blame, at the poor, infirm, meek and lame

They can't accept, won't accept the fact that we see them inept

But that's exactly what they are, from north to south to near and far

We put them there we pay their wage, now it's time for us to show our rage

This small proud nation must now rise and bring about their quick demise

There's only one way, have a guess? That's right my friends, you must vote YES!

Flowers of Westminster (Part One).

As the rosebud gently opens, it releases sweet perfume

And like the little child, its life begins to bloom

A life that's full of colour, bringing hope and love and joy

Innocent and beautiful, part of nature's rich employ.

So helpless and so tender, you killed that little dream

You tore their petals one by one as you listened to their screams

Then you cast them to the desert winds to a dry and arid land

To live in non-existence, forced by your evil hand.

Your selfish thoughts of lustfulness, made sure you never stopped

You pushed the life out from within, 'til the final petal dropped

A withered stem is all that's left and it shivers still with fear

Even now they see the evil men and those sounds they still can hear

You ripped the heart from life itself, you killed that life stone dead

Those young and happy vibrant years, are now a graveyard in your bed.

Flowers of Westminster (Part Two).

How does it feel to take a life, to kill a childhood dream

What is it like to silence joy, to hear a child scream?

Screams from boys just eight years old as you lead them to your bed

Can you remember how it felt or have you blocked that from your head?

Boys and girls forced out for play, how much did each one cost?

Did you think of them as human or all that they have lost

Did you think about their feelings or how much you made
them cry

Or the shame they have to live with, a life that's lived with
lies

But lies, you know all about them but know nothing about
shame

And though you know the guilty ones, you will never give a
name

And your good old dear will shut her mouth, the loyal
perfect wife

Prim and pretty, for the cause, will just get on with life

While those kids cried for their mothers, driven half insane

Were raped, slapped and tortured, screaming out in pain

Begging you for mercy as tears ran down their face

But you, you didn't give a damn, to beg was not their place

No, you had paid good money, you did as you pleased

Ravaging young children, it's you who are diseased

You abused your name, position, power and waved your
magic wand

And for a price your orphans came from London and
beyond

Oh! Paedophilia ruled supreme in your secret service, PIE

You bought the judges, paid their lunch, whilst kids were left to die

They died a death, are dying still, because they filled your needs

Hell is where you're heading for your Satanic deeds.

NO for YES.

Vote NO for YES to conscription

Vote NO for YES to Trident

Vote NO for YES to illegal wars

Vote NO for YES to paid prescriptions

Vote NO for YES to University fees

Vote NO for YES to Private Healthcare

Vote NO for YES to more austerity

Just say NO and join us to fight illegal wars

We'll not only make a fortune but we'll be your guarantor

We'll even buy more missiles to guard this wretched land

And feed you more austerity, begging hand to hand

Again we'll make more money as we demand of you conscription

And we'll make money from your Uni fees and you'll pay for your prescriptions

And all you folk who've saved for years working for your little pensions

We've stolen once and will again, just call it our retention

You know you're better with us and we'll be ecstatic if you stay

We'll do all of the above for you, come on now make our day

What is it you don't understand, why can't you just say NO?

A quick buck's all we're after, don't say you didn't know!

Brothers and Sisters.

(Thank you to, the controversial, Tommy Sheridan).

Those who live with hopes and dreams are those who will succeed

Those without, are being controlled, by a power fed by greed

Don't be fed the propaganda but delve in and find the facts

But some you think, who tell the truth, have papered over the cracks.

If you deal in facts and figures, you cannot go far wrong

For there's a man called Tommy Sheridan whose passion is so strong

He sweeps aside the nonsense, oh YES, we've seen him in debate

But on his own he's something else, the man's nothing less than great.

He stands up for his country, it's people, their beliefs

And to know that he is on your side brings a huge sigh of relief

A powerhouse of verve and nerve, steel is in his eyes

But compassion, if you've heard the man, will come as no surprise

His contributions legendary, his conviction even more

He'll vilify the liars, thieves, the ones we all deplore

He's a presence and commitment, who holds you in his hand

For his heart beats for our Scotland, independence he demands

But the media were out to get him and made his life a mess

And now this stalwart's been rejected by politicians voting YES

We wish him luck in his appeal and that he gets right back on track

He's the one we flock to see, as I said, he gives us facts!

The Hapless King.

Not so very long ago, in a place called Scotlandshire

There lived a wealthy nation whose dreams were to aspire

They wanted nothing special just a peaceful happy life

A place where children laugh and play, free of grief and strife.

But an evil King called David, from a distant tortured land

Stood upon his pulpit and issued his commands

From far off Mount Olympus, he began to preach

As faces etched in disbelief, listened to his speech

We love all Northern Britain and I have this one thing to say

Just call your friends and families, these Jocks have got to stay.

We need their gas and oil, we need their expertise

For if they go our cash won't flow so remember to say please.

As King of all Etonians, it was a speech meant to inspire

But as usual, the hapless one, gave a talk that would backfire

Yet again he sadly failed, to lift the spirits of his tribe

And once again resorted, to his favoured ploy, the bribe!

They've never seen a man like me who has no heart or soul

I'm a man who could do anything but show me first your gold,

I'm the smarmiest of bastards, the best you've ever seen

Just ask the general public, in that outpost Aberdeen!

In fact, they've never seen me, in that city full of Scots

All that tartan blinds me, I hate that kilted lot.

He then sent forth his envoy, Sir Gideon by name

To a single end in Scotlandshire, where he played the banking game

The Hooray Henry's fell for it as he slipped out the back door

And the cokehead squirmed his way back to Facebook's richest whore.

All Scotlandshire took umbrage at the cheek of one, self-crowned

And cried "You'll never take our freedom and never take our pound"

But King David mustered up a band, not seen for a hundred years

And vowed to sway all Scotlandshire and to put to death their fears

He said we'll have a parliament with more powers if devolved

He thinks we're buttoned up the back or have not, as yet, evolved

Don't let the King's men fool you and close to them your doors

Chase them from your doorstep back to their coke and whores.

Flying Under A Free Sky.

On the 18th off September, you can make your deadly purge

And with a vote for Independence, you'll rid our country's scourge,

Relieved of all your worries, freed from all your stress

Consider no more compromise, no bargaining, duress.

We've been stifled by hypocrisy, angered by aggressive lies

And when destiny comes calling, we'll give the Scots'
reply

We're a nation that has bared its soul and opened up its
heart

We are ready for a brand new world and we'll embrace our
brand new start.

No saboteurs, no hangers-on, or those we do not trust

They'll be severed by a thoughtful pen to rid a government
unjust

Use your vote and use it well, I beg do not refrain

And our Saltire, blue with silver cross, will fly free once
again.

Blood stained fields where Scotsman died, will rise from
where they fell

And with lost friends we'll remember but on them we must
not dwell

Nor let them sway opinion, love them as you may

It's your time and your children's and with your vote, we'll win the day.

We're not filled with grand illusions or deluded in our minds

We've seen the way they treat us, now let's break these ties that bind

Our heritage, our culture, is threatened as I write

But a vote for Independence will give us back our given rights.

You and Me.

I may not have a vote but am so proud to take part

And these writings I give you, I give from my heart

In this battle for Scotland, to free us at last,

May our forefathers bless us for a treacherous past.

Absolve us with favour and give us the grace

To hold our heads high and be proud of our race

And rely not on others, our decisions to make

But be rulers ourselves for our citizens' sake.

To have the belief, the strength and the verve

To overcome fears and strengthen our nerves

To banish our ghosts, phantoms and wraiths

To give us the hope, the courage and faith

To reclaim our land, to reclaim what's ours

Take back the wealth Westminster devoured

They can find other pockets to line with their greed

Then watch the sea border retreat to the Tweed

An historical moment we can govern ourselves

And the union we left can find out for themselves.

Those subsidies came not from their great London House

But a proud people's country they managed to rouse

For too long we've listened and watched as you failed

We're tired of a union disjointed, derailed

So we're taking back Scotland and setting it free

And when I say we, I mean you without me.

The Outsiders (Us).

There's a House down by the river

By dear old Father Thames

Allegedly things happen there

And alleged are the names.

Their servants flail and pour mair drink

Abused like big boys toys

Voluptuous the women were

But these men preferred the boys

The drunken orgy filled the halls

With drug fuelled laughing freaks

But Dave the Jesus, as he's know now,

Just turned the other cheek

He knew what he was doing

And showed his better side

As a friendly voice approached him,

Saying, let's both enjoy the ride.

Mair drink, mair drink, they shouted,

But the drink was in decline

But Jesus took their Highland Spring

And turned it into wine

The revellers were in full swing

As our hierarchy raved

Holding high their banners

Confirming Jesus Saves

But what goes on tour stays on tour

That's just the way we are

For silence is what makes us strong

So one word and you're barred.

The Outsiders need never know

Jesus then proclaims

They were born to love and trust us

And pay for our little games

Look around at what we have

We've got Heaven here on hell

And though The Outsiders can't be with us

We're shafting them as well!

They buy and furnish houses

And we just sign a dotted line

And if anyone ever pulls you,

I'll see to it you're fine

Relax and just enjoy yourself

And put your trust in me

And you can stop now what you're doing

And get up off your knees!

18th September 2014.

The soldiers here are ready with pamphlets in their hands

Out informing with the truth across this bonnie land

They fight for what they think is right, Westminster take note

They want Independence for their country in a democratic vote.

Three hundred years together, it's time for a divorce

Countries, cities don't exist, it's London that's the force

Four nations bound together are now on bended knee

And they're all looking North to Scotland, to watch it breaking free.

Your Project Fear can't cut it, we see through all your lies

And an Independent Scotland, will be Westminster's demise

The gravy train will be no more, there'll be nothing left to take

But we'll send you down a dram or two with Independence cake.

We're not anti-English; we've three hundred thousand here

And with every other nation, they'll give the biggest cheer

We're a nation in a country not built on fear and greed

Thanks for your concern but we've everything we need

We've imports, engineering with financial expertise

And the best of universities but we don't charge any fees

And when we keep our taxes, we'll be spoilt here with powers

And on the 18th of September, we can call this Scotland ours.

A free Scotland then will prosper, governed by our own

Your Houses full of Common Lords: Will you keep them or disown

Who'll pay for these and Trident, that nuclear metal mess

Or will you privatise it, like The People's NHS?

24 Hours in Parliament.

We don't want Trident moored up here, we want it now
displaced

And the Clyde or any other place doesn't want your nuclear
waste

But the world as we know it, would blow up in our face,

According to Lord Robertson but he's totally lost the place.

And Hague won't promote our whisky if Yes is what we
choose

If the carry out's too dear for you, buy our cheaper Irn Brus

The Commons like a drink or two, sipping on champagne

Whilst fondling half the bar staff, some are only weans!

Steaming on our hard earned cash, two hundred grand
they've spent

Drunken orgies, commonplace, and it's us they represent.

Another one let off in court, politicians blame the police

Fuck the victims, fuck the law, we'll do as we please!

The paedophiles, no longer scared, like the frauds that rip
us off,

Are forgiven by their master, Westminster is their trough.

The rules of law they play by don't apply to you and me

They're the perks of Government criminals, we know them as MPs.

In Australia Cameron feeds his soul on a vineyard's finest wines

Thirteen grand for his entourage and that money's yours and mines

But he also thinks he's Jesus and filled the good Lord's head with dread

He's binned the loaves and fishes, installing foodbanks there instead!

Westminster Love You....really!

Polls may lift our spirits but the Tories lift them more

For each time they try to put us down, it's us who seem to score

On facebook/twitter The Yes go forth but not on TV/Press

Why? They're in the pockets of Westminster and that's a bloody mess!

Can you hear the children cry or the silence of the dead

How much can a nation take? Filling folks with dread

Deaths you say! Oh come now, you're taking things too far

Are we? Your House of rules and policies have left this country scarred.

From Osborne's speech in Edinburgh spouting your demands

How you wouldn't share **your** currency should a Yes vote split our lands.

Then instead of being positive, you bullied us with threats

But they're idle like your promises; your forte lies in debts.

I said I wouldn't mention prostitutes or tables lined with coke

So forget I ever wrote that, it's probably just a joke

I mean can you imagine Osbourne, snorting Charlie with a whore

Naw! He's a good clean living man and only shafts the poor!

You've set a British record for putting people on the street

Evicted in their thousands yet you show nothing but conceit

Your crimes against humanity and the pain that you've inflicted

You've ripped the heart right out this land, where's your Promised Land predicted?

The Union will survive you say no matter what Scots vote

A nameless faceless person had the audacity to quote

It's an illegal referendum and we'll dictate if they vote YES

It's just tyranny from heartless men, who are they trying to impress?

Love us, hate us, what is it? You change from day to day

Your contemptuous House just carries on like a bankrolled cabaret

And how a vote for Independence would lead to dictatorship

Oh! How quickly you withdrew that before its censorship!

Poor Wee Jola.

There's a woman, name of Lamont, who won't play by the rules

She has fallen like the others, to the school of ridicule

Her friends have all gone with her and followed fate's command

Now none of them can care for their people or its land.

We all succumb to money but not so to a bribe

And from this land that bred them, they should unsubscribe

Harsh words are not needed to break immoral souls

We need her more than ever to help us win the polls.

Look not upon the outside to see where beauty lies

For inside there's a demon whom no-one should despise

We all know she's a traitor most thoughts are uncouth

But her words are instruMENTAL to bring on Scotland's youth.

Wee Jola tries her utmost, to put our people down

But once we're free, we'll send her back to dear old London town

It's what she always wanted, to be with all her peers

They'll welcome back with open arms, a Scottish souvenir.

A remnant of our history, a relic from the past

A memory from a distant time and one who was miscast

This is not genetics talking but a decision has been made

This is not because you're crazy or that your brain's decayed

It's a choice we'll have to live with you and your friends gone

It's a pity you won't see, a free Scotland hail its dawn.

Take That!

That Gary Barlow's wonderful

He makes us all look just like fools

We work like hell to pay our way

While he puts on gigs for charity

He's superclean but refuses to pay tax!

A wee agreement he did sign

It was a tax free service, much maligned

His advisor said it's crystal clear

I should know, I'm the Premier

I'm dodgier than any man you'll find.

So with his pal our big bad Dave

He thought of all the cash he'd save

A quick handshake showed his support

Now poor Gary's ending up in court

Tax free Gary was his favourite friend!

The Premier on news today

Still backed his Gary all the way

Come here my son, come here to me

You can keep your precious OBE

That's one we'll keep to ourselves!

I bet he won't make this a song

But if he did would that be wrong?

He could make it platinum

And clear his tax bill with his sum

And me, I would be famous after all

A Law Unto Themselves.

Cameron's involved with some lunatics and clowns

Even with the heavy team, they seem let him down:

And the world is going to end, in cataclysmic fashion

Lord, he almost is believable, bombing us with passion.

Brown's too busy mumbling, Darling's just a mess

And Iain Duncan Smith's AWOL, claiming benefits for stress

"Edinburgh's in England" another begs us stay

Two loonies from across the pond, their brains further away.

Johann Lamont's claim to fame, we haven't got a mind

At least we see what's going on, that one just acts blind

Eddie Izzard bombs along, smelling rather sweet

A future London Mayor but with us he can't compete.

Milliband is Thatcher now, he eyes up Eddie's frock

Clegg is holding big Ed Balls, Osbourne starts to mock

The Coke King of The Union wants an orgy for the day

So texts his favourite escort, who'll come if he will pay.

Never mind an escort, we'll get the waiters and the staff

It wouldn't be the first time, we've dropped a bloody gaffe!

Get the judges round here, bring the Lords as well

And the man we know as Jesus can lead us into Hell.

In Exiled Memory.

The stories told of Clearances, crofters sacked and shipped away

To foreign lands across the sea, sailed those who could not pay

Broken men and families, waved their last to Scottish shores

The place they loved, born and raised, they would see no more.

With tearful eyes and hollow hearts, unwanted now and filled with grief

Their footprints dug deep in the sand, drag slowly, forced to leave

Subservient to masters all, who're in turn, submissive to
their grief

Abandoned by the wealthy Lairds, who put cash and profits
before need.

Those sands of time have drifted by a tide that's turning fast

But let the pipes lay bare those eerie airs, let laments lay in
the past

The rogues they fear, they still are here, but this time we
won't be sold

We'll take the pride of those who died; our freedom's
richer than your gold

Let the Saltire soar, our Lion Rampant roar, let Scotland's
emblem wear our crown

Though the stakes are high, that day is nigh when Scots as
freemen walk this ground.

That Time Is Coming Soon.

Yer Hoose o' Commons took nae heed

An' like The Lords will soon be deid

Folks like you, we dinnae need
Ye know not dignity.

Some dwell upon oor ancient past
But like the present cannae last
The future's oors and coming fast
Victorious we'll be.

A Scotland free is oors tae share
Nae poverty, nae lack o' care
Oor hopes and dreams, they a' lie there
One voice we will be.

The fear ye fed was your demise
Yer London Hoose is fu' o' lies
Scots will rule 'neath Scottish skies
Where ane an' a' are free.

Come the month, the day, the hour

Scots will feast on new found power

We'll toast this nation, ower n' ower

We won with wi' Dignity!

Subterfuge.

(Alleged of course)!

It's the ruling House of Power but alas beyond its prime

Where ministers and hangers on, live with daily crime

It's a den of cunning people who know deception and intrigue

A sophisticated honeycomb, that's way beyond our league.

The alchemists have long since gone but there are crafts that still exist

And I can hear them thinking, Am I next on the list?

Every day, a new name. Every day a heavy sigh

Every day a cover up but no-one tells us why!

For grand theft they pay paltry fines and very seldom
sacked

And for paedophilia, there's a giant hush, as though
someone's been fracked

But out here in the real world, you get jailed for sex with
kids

But in those subterranean halls, they close all sexual lids.
No-one hears, no-one sees and no-one ever speaks

The whole ill-gotten human race that live there bloody
reeks

And the ones who've robbed a house or two, in this inner
city dwell

In cahoots, the lot of them, but no-one here will tell.

Sick! You think? You're bloody right, this is a disgrace

And every day their victims see that evil on their face

The judges know, and do their best, and the police must
have their say

But will they name these monsters? They still walk the streets today.

They have the balls to make new laws on what's wrong and right for them

These children, once so starry eyed, now live a life condemned

Ignored by those who make the laws and those who reinforce

But the kids still scream, to no avail, until their voice is hoarse.

They shout out loud in silence but walls, I'm told, have ears

So all you Lords and ministers, look out for your peers

But more than that, look out for us, we're watching every case

And very soon, we'll name and shame, your evil guilty face.

They ridicule all others yet won't deal with what's within

There are criminals still roaming free in the UK's House of Sin

So be careful what you wish for when September comes around

It's not only what you see above but what else lies 'neath the ground.

Do you really want a Government over which no-one has control?

Cast a vote for Independence and bare your Scottish soul

And fear not the fear of failure but find courage in your heart

We're not better off together, now's the time for us to part.

Thousands lined the streets of Perth to say farewell and thanks you to one of Scotland's greatest politicians, and a hero to many, Alex Salmond.

The Vital Spark.

(A tribute to the great Alex Salmond).

In the fight for Independence, a young man made his name

Seen as treachery, in other's eyes, in Scotland he gained fame

A man who's willing to stand up and fight against their lies

A man who fights for all your rights and yet you criticise.

Not knowing him by meeting but by looking at his face

Or by the way he smirks or grins or lacks that certain grace

There is confident and arrogant, these words are poles apart

But he has abundance in the former, displayed with a rampant Scottish heart.

Many fall and don't get up, to box their final round

But this man he is the heavyweight and always stands his ground

He's fighting for his country yet planning against wars

Against the nuclear missiles here, based on Scotland's shores.

He's fighting for the right to live, free, to rule our own

A country, where the people, proud, feel they're all alone

Compelled he felt, duty bound, to challenge industries

Rife with every bias known, to bring us to our knees.

A man who'd not be brainwashed but studied facts instead

A man who bowed to no-one and filled his foes with dread

A man who reaches higher still, fighting for our cause

A man who fights for Scotland's rights and yet wants no applause.

A man who's for democracy, self-governance and peace

A man who wants the taxes dropped and poverty to cease

It should be every man's ambition to ease the hurt and pain

But some men they want everything when there's nothing left to gain.

Death, destruction, is their aim, as they wallow in their greed

A lustful life devoid of soul, and of shame, they take no heed

It's against these very people this man speaks out loud

He is not a saint by any stretch, but a man, and one who's proud.

Proud to be of Scottish stock and proud to be a Scot

Saying what we can do if we're free, and not, what we cannot

His anger shows when we're put down or those who show contempt

But the wrongs they speak are put to rights, rendered as exempt.

You will never sway this Scotsman's love and the faith in what he says

His own beliefs in a Scotland free are deserving of our praise

When the tabloids print or the media state their biased views unkind

Be certain that the answers dealt, are with Scotland foremost in his mind.

Thirty Years.

Silence flows from a wordless mouth, our ears turned cutely off

We see his face but hear no words and yet, him, we must scoff

His presence gives not ambience but fills the air with hate

Elected by, and for us all, he ignores us to dictate.

The race is on to jot down notes, to scribble words he's said

Or scrolling back to freeze a frame that's stuck inside your head

You've snapped the picture on your phone and thought your comments through

Then Facebook, Twitter comes alive with a multitude of views.

We scramble now like lunatics alerting all our "friends"

Our thoughts no longer are our own as we trawl through texts and Trends

Our voice is heard through written words and scattered worldwide

We are no more the silent voice, the net's our newfound guide.

This guide's corrupt, controlling all but the truth is out there too

And those lies of 30 years ago prompt grievances anew

The secret papers inform us now, blatantly they lied

Why must we stay united when a Government has no pride?

Corrupt, deceitful beings, lying through their teeth

So look not at the talking head but at the monster underneath.

This Governing Farce.

We're only a number, a pawn in their game

A piece on their board with no face and no name

Our faith doesn't matter or colour of skin

What's important to them is this game they must win.

Fat politicians grow richer each day

And each day their public are wasting away

A third world Britain that used to be Great

Now the poor who have nothing, have less on their plate.

Large supermarkets throw food out as waste

And the hungry queue up, they've acquired the taste

For stealing food out of date even though it's gone stale

But it's enough for our police force to throw you in jail.

Food Kitchens flourish in this land once so proud

But you still cannot hear though we shout it out loud!

We once joined the army for three meals a day

A trip overseas with full pension and pay

Now the soldiers who serve us don't rush to get back

Because walking our streets brings the threat of attack.

This monster in Britain has no face or no name

Willing to kill but they won't accept blame

Riots are rife and bring on more deaths

While the government puff 'til they run out of breath.

What have we done and where do we go?

At least it's a truth when they say they don't know

But confronting the truth is not what they're all about

Deceptive and frightened they've ALL been found out

It's the cheats who're in politics who should be on the dole

What's happened to Britain, I guess it's been sold.

Is This Our Matrix?

There's no such thing as clean fresh air,

They spread pollution everywhere,

They control our wagging tongues

And the chemicals put in our lungs

The controllers will not touch these pills,

They know that each one brings more ills

But the money laundering pharmacies

Hide cures for every known disease.

If one is found they create some more,

They see money flow from every pore

Our money spent is all controlled,

They'll give us pounds but hold back gold

Happy, sad, rich or poor,

They determine lives by peace and war

Mass destruction, atrocities

The unemployed, the poverty

They control what's bought and what's to be sold

From the births of young to the deaths of old.

It's a bankers' bank run by the few

Who tell us what to say and do,

They give us rope to hang ourselves

We're only sheep and they, the wolves,

They let us think that we are free

But we're always crouched on bended knee

Obeying fashions they demand

Their wish is just a bleak command.

They watch you everywhere you go

Your every step and all you know

Financiers who know their craft

Destroying us with overdrafts

They have us where we all should be

As they control, who's bound, who's "free"

Absolving those whose backs have bent

Whilst monitoring each penny spent

Do they control all that we see?

Is our factual, mystery?

And these idyllic lands with bright blue skies

Are they just a Matrix in our eyes?

Why must we stay united when a Government has no pride?

Corrupt, deceitful beings, lying through their teeth

So look not at the talking head but at the monster underneath.

A Date with Independence.

When King James V1 of Scotland, united with the English crown

Our lords for lands betrayed us to, far off London town

We still placed hopes upon them, which, in hindsight wasn't fair

For the last thing on Westminster's mind, was for us to have our share.

The Famine that struck Ireland, where a million lives were lost

Didn't happen here in Scotland for other Scotsmen bore the costs

No help came from Westminster, not one penny did they give

To them we were a burden, they cared not if we died or lived.

And what of The Highland Clearances where towns just disappeared

Millions forced to leave a land, a Scotland they revered

Again this was for money where sheep cost less than men

And when they closed the shipyards, it happened once again.

Billions they have taken, our resources they have used

To pay off Thatcher's debtors and still we're being abused

You now have the chance to change it, your life, your destiny

Vote YES for independence or else face more agony.

Do we need the Tories tell us, how to run our beloved land

When decisions made in London do not meet Scots' demands

This is not about a monarchy or a vote about a throne

But to reclaim back the land we love and to govern as our own.

They've given us our foodbanks which we know the proud will snub

But a minister from Parliament says, we spend the savings down the pub

How out of touch, these Tories are and Labour's not that far behind

With them this is Scotland's future and it's a future much maligned.

The money owed by Britain is at an all time high, that's fact

Paid for by Scotland's oil, whisky, each Scottish worker's tax

Why do we pay more to the taxman, when we get less in return

If you vote to stay united then you can watch your country burn.

If you're wondering why there's nothing here to back the other side

It's because they've answered nothing or tripped up when they've lied

If UNITED means we're stronger, you couldn't be more wrong

Just look at what the last few years have brought and say that you belong.

It's a country more divided by class than borderlines

The rich are getting richer whilst the poor are left behind

The NHS in Scotland is the one the rest are looking to

We've a country full of riches with personnel to see us through

This is not for Alex Salmond, it's for the future of this land

For men, women, children who want to make a stand

If you're still undecided, please just don't take a wild guess

Put your X where you know is right, in the box that's written YES.

I'm not a politician but with these eyes I see

Destruction, degradation on a scale we could not foresee

I look around at fellow Scots, ones who built these lands

Britain may have ruled the waves but those ships were built by Scottish hands.

Everything Is Alright.

They say that Hitler killed himself but that Nazi's here to stay

He's born again, a woman, and come back as Theresa May

She'll strip and terrorise you and her next move's not a tease

Then persecute you, God knows how, when you are on your knees.

Is Hitler's new found ally really just a guy?

Or is she a reincarnation, well, she's got the Fuehrer's eyes

This benefits her colleagues as they watch on, enthralled

Just who wears the trousers and who's got the biggest balls?

She's eradicating terrorists by removing British passports

And this will leave them stateless with no help from any courts

But what about Westminster's lot? They've left us in a state

-Less half of our treasury, they used for their estates.

Are they then not terrorists, an international threat

Waging wars for money's sakes whilst increasing national debts?

Is Blair another Hitler? No! At least Hitler had the guts

And if he was here alive today, he'd lead these bloody nuts!

But he'd have to battle Charlie, who thinks he's Putin's double

Less has started world wars, this future King is trouble

He lives up to his father's name, his gaffes are world renowned

God help this bloody country when Charlie boy is crowned!

Country First.

I know it's a democracy with a democratic vote

But do you realise what you've done to us because you took no heed or note

You just voted in a party that wants to end our Scottish rule

Holyrood may be no more and be ruled by London's fools.

You hadn't the guts to meet him, you stood not by his side

And when Scots rebuked his every word, you felt the need to hide

We're whingeing junkies, scroungers, they'll take us out of the EU

Extremist's words against the Scots, do you share that point of view?

The future of this country, relies on knowledge that you've gained

Being uninformed is laziness and your like will still be chained

We're pawns in Westminster's chess game where pawns are all despised

Stop listening to the media, their words only chastise

There are people sweating blood and tears making sure that you're well versed

So put aside your differences, your bigotry, and for once put Scotland first

We're sick of all this hatred and your songs of love and hate

This is Scotland's time, your children's time and it's you who'll seal their fate!

Would be Politicians.

It frightens me they've got a vote

But they haven't got a clue

They go on about corruption

Yet they're corrupted too,

Influenced by family, friends,

Who themselves don't understand

And yet they tell us of their love

They have for their land.

And it all comes down to Salmond

The man they love to hate

This egoist, dictator,

How they'd love to put him straight.

They're like the fan of football

Who's never kicked a ball

Nor made a speech in their whole life

But want that final call.

The Greatness of Britain.

A game of chance, Monopoly or a deadly game of thrones

We don't know which party's which, all parties now are clones

Your colours Yellow, Red and Blue, we once knew who was who

But you're colours fed each other's beds and left a messy hue.

You're causing deaths through ignorance, did you hear me, Deaths!

You're being cursed right at the end with the poorest's dying breaths

You're too busy playing games, always blaming one another

Then as pals, sell our assets off, you would sell your sister's mother!

You starve the poor so they'll find work and sling them off the dole

While you enjoy your canapés with our money that you stole

There'd be no need for charity if you all paid bloody tax

Instead you see their heads on blocks as you wield the corporate axe.

Kids are running round the streets searching for a daily meal

And the coppers that would that would feed them, you decide to steal

To buy new curtains, buy a house or lay a brand new lawn

As their mothers take their wedding rings, to survive they have to pawn

Survive I said, Not Live! Do you even know they're there?

World War 11 and handouts, that's how it's being compared,

Everything is at a price, excepting death, which comes as free

Then you promise we'll have everything, if you only vote for ME!

Well we voted and we never got, all we got was you

With a spineless, feeble Cabinet, who haven't got a clue

At some point in your existence, you must have taken note

But then again, you never have and will never get our vote.

When a racist, fascist party take over your command,

You can tell me when you wake up, where went your
pleasant land

You can shout from London's rooftops across your prized
Stockbrokers Belt

For the more you shout, the less we hear, we'll not be
bloody telt!

You're arrogant, obnoxious and as smarmy as they come

And although we don't share your school tie, don't think us
Scots are dumb.

As employees you should listen but that's not what you
want to hear

But instead you punish citizens who already live in fear

You'd the power of position but you kept that Tory trait

Of thinking big but playing small whilst still thinking
Britain Great.

Esther McVey.

She's the darling of Tories now the other one has gone

Sent packing by his masters, they just bring on the next clone

This one's their blonde haired beauty; they think a work of art

Just a soulless, skirted puppet with a politician's heart.

Her brightly coloured dresses hide a very dim lit brain

And in any other business, she'd be labelled as insane

She's a closet human being still not ready to come out

As she shows us every day in life and leaves us in no doubt!

It's like an elocution lesson when she's asked for an oration

In almost sexual exploration, her lips seek out adoration

That mouth of her twists around 'til her words seem out of sync

But I bet it comes in handy when she's slamming down free drink.

She's the one responsible for writing her own scripts

So don't be fooled by her silky hair and those wandering ruby lips

Some say her rambling letters make some audacious claims

She wants to see you suffer and that's every Tories aim.

Meeting Alex Salmond.

I wrote this next one on the plane coming back from
Glasgow to London and had the good fortune to meet Alex
Salmond as he flew down from Edinburgh, at Heathrow. I
walked over to him and apologised for interrupting his
conversation and said: Mr Salmond, I just want to wish you
all the best in the referendum. I then told him I didn't have
a vote as I lived in London. His reply: "Ah! But you can
always keep a good hoose"! We had a wee chat and then I
left. I went through the airport doors for a cigarette and
remembered about the poem I'd just written on the plane. I
ran back and asked him to sign the paper but he asked me
what it was, I told him a poem about Indy. His entourage
had started to move away but he called them back and
indicated that he was talking to me! He asked whilst
reading when I'd done it and I said just now, on the plane.
He looked at me and said "When? Now? I said yes and to
prove it asked him to turn the poem over. It was my
boarding pass. He asked if he could keep it, I said yes, of
course but wanted a photo of it first as it was my draft. He
then asked one of the young ladies with him for a business
card and asked me if I would send it to him. Then he gave
me a signed copy of The White Paper and we went our
ways. He did however mention that they are going on eBay
for £150.00 – it's still here Mr Salmond! I sent the poems
to him and he sent a letter back, signed, which is now
framed and sitting proudly in my living room. He was the
first to read this and so this particular poem is a wee bit
special to me. Alex Salmond is a real gentleman but when
he goes to work, he is fighting for us!

Set Scotland's Children Free.

Though we gang thegither blind

With hope in heart, our faith we'll find

All doubts we'll cast and leave behind

To bring our future home.

The land that shaped our history

Will now define our destiny

And set us free from tyranny

Our country we shall rule.

Willingly we face our fate

Escape the claws of a Britain Great

And free a nation not a state

Free from poverty.

An ethnic race we're in their eyes

Scotland's dream they all despise
But Scotland's people yet can rise
And show the world we care.

A nation locked, a nation chained
Their changing laws left unexplained
These ministers can't be ordained
The wrath of Hell must die.

These idiots see us the fool
And think us Scots unfit to rule
If Britain shines then we're the jewel
We've paid our way and more.

Sold by rogues this country drowns
A piece of gold to share a crown
Now we've the chance to turn that 'round
A cross is all it takes.

Heritage and culture, pride

We'll shape our future, turn the tide

It's you as Scots who must decide

Give your kids a chance.

A Scottish Darling?

Hey Darling, tell us is it true, yer buildin' oan Faslane?

I'm sure the Scots wid rather huv mair nurseries fur their weans!

Ah mean they need a nursery and they cannae walk tae Bute

An' if they couldnae buy weans pampers, they'd hae nappies made fae jute!

An' Darling, wull there be a war, is there a nuclear plant being built?

An' Darling, a wee wummin said, if ye win ye'll ban the kilt!

Ah hope ye didnae mean that an' ah hope it isnae true

Fur a wummin's life is nothin' when she gets the answers withoot clues!

Darling, why do you want unity with a land of hills and deer?

Don't tell me, it's that Hadrian's Wall, for you're living still in fear.

It wisnae Scots that built it, we welcome a' wi' pride

It wis built upon the English soil cos it's pointed oan their side.

Oh! Darling, I have fantasies but I shouldn't really say

But in 9 months time, expect some news, a surprise is on its way,

Was it a pregnancy you thought of? Well it wouldn't be the dole

But it's you who's just been shafted as you sold out on your soul.

You imbecile, you traitor, you're the one who's going down

You and your buddy Cameron are just a pair of clowns

He tries to run a country; the man could not run a bath

And his figure work for Scotland's wrong, he should have studied Maths.

The words you say just don't stack up and half your truths are lies

And we, in bonnie Scotland, will drink to your demise,

You may have fooled the Tories but we're an educated lot

And it takes more than a premier, to con a bloody Scot!

Big Guns and Damp Powder.

They've brought their heavy, Gordon Brown

To pave the way for yet more clowns

But the more they send to tell us No

The more we'll tell them where to go

And leave JoLa behind, she always makes us laugh!

He'll give it everything he's got

Then remember he was once a Scot

He's a Tory in a boiler suit

And all he wants is Scotland's loot

To buy more friends like Dave on Facebook sites!

The more they lie, the more it seems

We'll realise all our hopes and dreams

With every No speech comes success

As the undecided switch to Yes

Bring the big guns, cannon fodder all!

He gave us hope based on our oil

Then gave Westminster all our spoils

Now says we'll have powers over tax

Aye Right! No more bullshit, give us facts

You should have done that when you had the chance!

This man sold Scotland down the Thames

As he bedded Tories and Lib-dems

Then chuckled with his good mate Blair

They'll take the bait, leave Trident there

Scotland's been so very good to us!

And of Faslane's radiation leak

SEPA silent but were forced to speak

As Chernobyl raced through our minds

They thought The Simpson's more aligned

Now The ex New York Mayor wants us free!

As for Boris, that man's just a laugh

With every speech there comes a gaffe

A pound spent in Croydon helps Glasgow

He's the star of London's Lord Mayor Show

And his schoolboy friend's the one who rules our land.

Independence.

There are millions claimed in benefits from Downing Street
alone

By our elected puppeteers sitting on their plastic thrones

Yet they're stopping housing hand-outs to those under
twenty five

But maybe they just want them dead cos they cost too much
alive!

The bedroom tax is losing pace and actually costing more

Ten million lost to start with and new loopholes found
galore

And those rebates mean more paperwork and with that
comes more costs

So add to that ten mil deficit, another five mil loss!

No free meals for Scots children said the Labour Party
chiefs

Let them use our foodbanks and compound their Scottish
grief

But we'll still push it through in England, because we deserve the best

And when we've milked it for our own, we'll feed the bloody rest!

In London's Fire Service, ten more stations were closed down

Vote NO and we will follow suit in this circus led by clowns

They conjured up weird figures then hit us with more tax

But I wish for once they'd tell us all, not lies, but truthful facts!

Our Date with Destiny.

White Papers 30 years old now have unleashed what we all knew

That the governments of yesteryear have been robbing me and you,

Modern day Robin Hoods but it was their own pockets that they lined

And the Cabinet that sat back then were of Anti-Scottish mind.

Do you think they're any different now, if you do then you're a fool

Wake up to Westminster's silence, the home where Corruption rules!

Do you want these suits in London, controlling our affairs

Scots ,Welsh, Irish, English, all rich through treasury shares

And a Scot, who kept his mouth shut, a Judas to the core,

Watched them raise the tax in Scotland, and no doubt went back for more!

Oh yes, they'll paint a pretty picture, of Scotland in control

But all we'll get's more poverty, foodbanks and the dole

What's next? Maybe a means test, more rises in our tax

They're going to raise flight duty, to hit our tourism, that's fact.

I see the streets of London daily; don't think they're paved with gold

They're consumed with upright beggars where the young live with the old

Shabby coats replace the suits, a doorway for a home

And nightly they're just moved along 'til there's nowhere left to roam

The drugs, the muggings, wasted lives, the increasing unemployed

This daily life in Britain, where souls have been destroyed

We're warned in leafy suburbs, don't go out after dark

For the muggers they will get you and they'll do you for a lark

A woman is no different, for age they do not care

Hacked or beaten, in their homes, if united, this we share.

They hide this from us in the news and report on wars worldwide

They surely can't believe it's perfect when there's such a great divide.

They don't want to scare the tourists or don't want to admit

That the people running Britain are truly that unfit!

And it is growing, getting worse, they can't control the crime

In Scotland we'd do better with our own money given time

And I know that we're no angels, but do we want to be a part

Of a Britain that is crumbling, governed by an ice-cold heart?

They see us a third world country, like a backroad out of town

A land that when they've raped us, will kick us when we're down

We're down just now for God's sake, open up your eyes

Westminster only knows one way and that's filling you with lies.

They'll make sure that with a No vote we'll be gone and lost forever

And by that time, it'll be too late, no matter our endeavour.

We're the only country EVER, to fund our own collapse

For our fortunes went to pay their debts whilst we fed on the scraps

And what of Traitor Darling, on prime time news tonight

The voice of Better Together, like the Devil quoted rights

How Scotland gains with unity, how lovely it will be;

In truth we'll be divided more then be begging on our knees.

And what of the opposition, when will they get their say?

Well, the corrupt, one sided BBC, never answered that today!

September's Song.

September's song will bring to us some voices in disguise

Media will let us hear just what they're told to say

Scaremongering is just a game, they're politicians' lies

Lame threats come, but they soon die, each and every day.

What will happen to the Union's wares, when the blue has disappeared?

Will the rUK bail out the shops that sell these souvenirs?

A fire sale on giant scale selling tat once so revered

A changing land won't change that much, it still will be austere!

And what about the EU, with Scotland on its own

Will the rUK, as Scotland must, have to re-apply?

The UK signed that dotted line to join the Euro zone

Yet no answers come from anyone, to the Scottish question, why?

The calculating Cameron knew the outcome all along

He'll lose the Independence vote then head straight to the polls

Europe doesn't matter so why should he prolong

To live under this master's rule, where he is just a troll.

The secrets that you kept from us, paedophiles et al

Breaches to security of an aide you trust the most

You let him write the children's code to boost parents' morale

Yet you denied all knowledge and for that you'll pay the cost.

The Family of Nations.

The most powerful man in Britain brought his forces north

The conference for Scots Tories but no one here burst forth

The empty seats told stories of Scotland's love affair

With a party and its leader, who have lost the will to care!

A packed hall was expected with a thousand here or more,

Were they out spending expenses in some posh department store?

His words look good on paper but we've heard it all before

It's time to end this Union with a cross not blood and gore.

On the UK Cameron stood up and with hand on heart he said

It's the birthplace of the NHS, the BBC and Christian Aid,

Well the first they're going to privatise, the second they control

And the third condemns their foodbanks and say the Tories have no soul.

We are The Family of Nations, Cameron boldly said

But if Independence follows, Theresa May said this instead

She's his partner in the No side yet wants border barricades!

Will our checkpoints then be guarded with gunmen on parade?

Why do they want to keep us if Scotland is a drain?

To stay part of this Union would be claiming Scots insane

And whilst the rich steal off the poorest, we need a Robin Hood

Well you've one right here in Edinburgh and its name is Holyrood!

The Iron Lady, Long May You Rust.

(For The Queen Bitch herself).

We remember all our shipyards laced along the Clyde

'Til the Iron Lady closed them and took away men's pride

British steel and coal were sold yet she had no regrets

Then raped our North Sea Oil to pay off Britain's debts.

Civil war had entered Britain, now a decimated land

As riots raged, the angry crowds, took the law in their own hands

Poverty was everywhere with handouts commonplace

As lies poured from a mouth of steel, a lady without grace

The working class got in her way, we were worse than scum

As the rich afforded every taste, the poor lived off their crumbs

Britain had a Hitler who brought a country to its knees

And with a cabinet full of yes men, ruled with consummate ease,

She was right no matter what and never ever would concede

But the tyrant with the iron fist, sacked those who disagreed.

She changed political boundaries to help her Tories win more votes

But Scotland stood united, I wish the rest had taken note

And education changed as well as she reformed Scotland's role

As educationalists watched on in vain, we were cast onto the dole

Britons could not wait to party as her death came on the news

It seems to me that every class have aired their common views?

The Pen and The Sword.

Is Cameron too hard-line, they're now baying for his head

There's no doubt that he lives in fear, Scotland fills this man with dread

He's afraid of Independence, to face Salmond on stage

But when he spoke from London's velodrome, his brain had disengaged.

He then turned his eyes to Europe, with aides being sent to Spain

His rolling eyes flipped pound signs and how much he stood to gain

Westminster don't see people, they just see Scottish notes

It's no wonder that in Scotlandshire, the Union wants your votes.

The English, Welsh and Irish asked: Is what he's doing right?

The Scots are saying: Bring them on; we're ready for the fight

Each day another saga, each day a new debate

You tried to draft in Putin but left out The United States

These are criminals and killers and you're playing to their hand

And if the NO vote carries through, what will be their demands?

Free entry into Scotland, nuclear lessons for the insane

It will be Chernobyl all over but this will be Faslane!

Our weapons of destruction aren't wholly owned by us

America owns most of these and you think: What's the fuss?!!

They're allowed to place the nuclear waste, with the emphasis on "place"

A change of word and by EU law, their poison is displaced

One word and all your rights are gone, our coastline is alive

With no investigation, no life there now will thrive.

We can change this coastline and use this shifting tide

Though days are running out my friends, time is on our side

Do not look through empty eyes, you do not stand alone

We're taking back what's rightly ours, like Kings upon our thrones

Free to rule the land we love, free from London's chains

We're free to break the shackles to free us from these pains

I look around my Scotland and am blessed with what I see

The richest landscape ever known, a land God gave to me

I live in hope for all of us, I do not live in fear

My mind is strong and focused, my vision it is clear

I've dreamed that dream a thousand times, it lives inside of me

And now Scotland has that power, to set its children free

This is not being Nationalistic, rebellious or romantic

It is not being anti-English but is being democratic

It's not about a party or even just one man

It's all about the Scottish, ruling Scotland's land

It's ridding what we've had so far, in more three hundred years

Living off Westminster's scraps and failing in our fears

I know I'm not a lonely voice and this is not a dreamer's view

It's a vote change to a system and what the old one's done to you,

I never understood the proverb, the pen is mightier than the sword

But now I understand completely, the meaning of these words.

The Traitors' Pit.

Their entrance is a garden

Filled with fauna, flora

But what lurks inside is a deep, dark side,

Is a Sodom and Gomorrah.

So welcome to The Traitors' Pit

Where the wolves care not whose blood they spit

With caviar they sip champagne

Oblivious to our suffering, pain

And as broken dawns greet the poor

They see us as rich men's whores!

Pumped for every cent they've got

An early grave's the poor man's lot

Another cash flow law enforced

Whilst exempting all their own, of course.

The master rules the lion's den

In Downing Street at No 10

With brain alert and eyes wide shut

They look not for famine or for glut

But for selfish glory, greed and power

And why we must take back what's ours.

YES!

Generations going back centuries gave us stories of the past

Where Scots went into battle, not needing to be asked

They fought then for their freedom, so many gave their lives

And with that life, ensured that we, as a nation would survive.

From The Declaration of Arbroath to recent legal wars we've fought

No nation in the world today are reputed like The Scots.

This year will be a battle, not fought with sword or gun

But it's the battle of all battles and one that must be won.

If our forefathers had this chance for a bloodless victory

They would take it in an instant just to set their Scotland free

Or will their deaths mean nothing? It was us they died to save

Instead of that we argue, as they look on from turning graves,

Rise up you sons and daughters; put an end to this regime

It's time to answer Scotland's calling and realise our dream.

We have always told our stories of a rich and gory past

Of battles won, defeated, we've a history unsurpassed

Yet this silent war we're fighting still has a warring crowd

But you can give yourself, your children, a reason to be proud

With the ownership of country, one to govern as our right

And for generations yet to come, have a future that is bright.

BBC Bias Intro.

I was asked to put the following out by Moira Williams who was organising the first BBC BIAS demonstration. She was out walking, with no access to a laptop/computer so I put this out for her. I know it's not a poem but felt it was important enough to put in. This is what I wrote on Facebook which fired up hundreds, eventually thousands to attend:

PLEASE SHARE WITH EVERYONE YOU KNOW.

YES CAMPAIGNERS are organising a peaceful protest outside BBC Glasgow this Sunday, 1st June, at midday.

They have asked that everyone shares this post to ensure optimum turnout.

THE YES BUS WILL BE THERE.

This is a protest against BBC bias and the omission of relevant facts. People are suitably sickened by the BBC and this week, we will have our chance to tell them how we feel and how they are ruining this referendum with their Westminster leanings.

Please bring a Herald if you have one and if you have more than one, please bring them along to share to highlight our strength, the power we actually have and to let them know we have had enough. Thank you.

BBC Bias.

(For everyone who went today in silent protest, 1st June 2014.).

It's equality, parity, truths that we want

And not words construed from We Can to We Can't

We want speeches and figures, confrontation, debate

With informed discussions to decide Scotland's fate.

The people of Scotland relied on your news

But your warped, twisted versions made us seek other views

Your malevolent comments, this spirit, won't break

But our Scottish pride's taken all it can take.

You're found guilty of bias, a fact you deny

You can't keep ignoring as cruel barbs fly

You're running on empty with your fuel denied,

Independence is coming and truth's on our side.

Your prejudice reeks of Unionist tone

It's akin to apartheid and should not be condoned

Our history, language, removed from our schools

And our culture condemned by minority rule.

But the spirit of Scotland is something to fear

And the rise of a nation and people's now here

Have pride on yourself and let your heart soar

For a free Scotland will prosper like never before.

Scots are renowned for their courage and fight

So free up your mind and claim back your right

The future of Scotland is your destiny

It's freedom for Scotland, your chance to be free.

Nobody Wants You!

(Words to the famous tune made immortal by The Alexander Brothers, NOT wee Dougie and Danny I hasten to add, for a BBC Bias protest).

Two thousand Yessers standing

In a packed Pacific Quay

Protesting on corruption

Of a bias BBC

A grassroots crowd had gathered

And when I asked them why

They turned with fire in their eyes

And all as one they cried:

We're sick of your bias

Tired of your lies

Your house of corruption

Yessers despise

Keep all your kisses

And save all your tears

None of us want you

Now who's filled with fear?

The people here with children

Are here for more than show

They want to tell The BBC

Exactly where to go

For once we're Independent

You'll come back on your knees

And then we'll say you had your chance

You're no more our Licensee.

We're sick of your bias

Tired of your lies

Your house of corruption

Yessers despise

Keep all your kisses

And save all your tears

None of us want you

Now who's filled with fear?

The World Has Changed.

Come Nazi, come fascist, come racist from Hell

Come all homophoebics, come Ukip as well

The impact you made, we could never foretell

There's a hatred that burns deep inside you

Your bitterness mimics a black magic spell

The times have already changed.

Would you demonise Catholics and castrate the Jews?

Won't somebody tell them it's not deaths they should choose

And those foetal abortions are their sickening views

What kind of world do they live in?

We'd better wise up we have nothing to lose

The times are already changing.

An immigrant's married your dear mother's son

But it's too late to undo what is already done

For man loving man was there when time begun

And a cure will never be found

Accept that you're wrong, let the world live as one

For these times are constantly changing.

As the war rages on your myths are dispelled

And those houses you drank in have seen you expelled

You were born in the gutter and there you still dwell

You're exposed in the blink of an eye

As you sleep with your partners, it's contempt that you sell

Get off, our world is changing.

The world's an asylum ruled by lunatics

And those statements you gave us you now contradict

You laid your foundations buy ran out of bricks

Your temple's decaying and dying

And those drugs that you sought could now be your next fix

This time we'll make the change.

Your Choice!

Devolution's a gift for the present; can we trust them to think it will last?

For centuries they've only taken, look to their inglorious past

From The Union that promises riches be very afraid of their fee

So when Liberty calls, embrace it, it's your sovereign right to be free.

Their ever quickening promise of Devo, will be just as quickly reversed

It's another play set down in London with every character, move well rehearsed

In the longest run play between nations, this Union has never been fair

They're adept at any acceptance but debts are all they ever will share.

Westminster would love to disown us, they see us degenerate sons

But their politicians need funding and they're armed with political guns

Firing their love north to Scotland, smothering Scots with their mirth

These same men and women betrayed us by betraying the land of their birth.

For 400 years they've eroded, a culture, a nation, a race

Scotland, our country is dying, their intention, it should not be replaced

And it's right you should fear for your future, your own future is yours to decide

The Prize: the re-birth of our nation, its people, its culture, its pride.

A Scots' Parliament full of stalwarts, a free Scotland, they hope to reign

Where truths push them onward for freedom, with lies they have nothing to gain,

Success has never come easy, it's all down to the choices we make

But to have that one chance to be free once again, is a chance we should all readily take.

Dear Barrack Obama.

(This was actually sent to Barrack Obama at The White House but funnily enough, he never wrote back).

Your Declaration of Independence, drawn up, by proud Scottish hands

Against a British government Our Fathers fought, so you could be free in your land

Signed by brave men in thick Scottish blood, signed for thousands who did not survive

Did they die so that you, Mr President, could see Scotland's freedom denied?

You'll say those words were misconstrued, misplaced, misused, abused

But you bowed to a man, a sneak, liar and cheat, ignorance is never excused

The land of the free would rather keep us in chains, pandering to a weakest request

Like a novice, caught off your guard when this matter, you should not have addressed

Awareness is a political trait, yet you Sir, were caught unawares

But atonement is never too late to bring balance to Scottish affairs.

This should not have been mentioned, but too late, the damage is already done

As your pro-Union claim claims a victory, their spin is already spun

But whether secretly contrived or if, genuinely, you were surprised

We blame you for your choice of words, you immorally comprised

But this is Scotland's time to stake our claim and truths will always conquer lies

And on the 18th of September we'll take freedom and have no need for compromise.

On The Rise.

As we battle for health they're fighting for wealth

Charging like bulls with their usual stealth

If we govern ourselves, yes there'll be mistakes

But they'll be our own, not what Westminster makes

We're protesting against a government's that's wrong

Their constant denials have gone on far too long

No more this oppression or feeling suppressed

We'll get rid of the gloom and the constant unrest

There's an explosion in hope, a step up in pride

With an army of people who stand side by side

From every background, race, colour and creed

Their confidence growing they aim to succeed

Inspired by values, they're inspiring others

Fathers, mothers, sisters and brothers

With foot soldiers rising they're taking the fight

Through villages, cities and citing what's right.

This is our challenge and we will stand our ground

Dispelling the myths, pulling barriers down

Conferring, debating with an even exchange

This our platform, our catalyst for change

Standing as one with potential and hope

And the whole world agrees that the Scottish will cope

Collectively pulling for what's right and what's fair

Ensuring our riches are commonly shared

To heighten our prospects, our status enhance

By grasping the power and seizing this chance

We can rid Scotland's injustice and social unrest

Which the Better Together has failed to address!

What Is Going On?

Their brains are barred from logic as they speak of "blood and soil"

And our resources are a burden, especially that of oil

Wouldn't every state and nation love to bear this onus

But what they see as "everything" is to Scotland, just a bonus!

Yet we haven't seen one cent of this as Westminster takes it all

And so strange it's not a burden when it's them who make the call.

The Queen's declined from answering, Cameron's United plea

Twice he's asked Her Majesty to keep Scotland from being free

There will be no "Obama Moment" from the Queen, our head of State

As her ministers in Edinburgh advised: "stay out of this debate".

The Pope refused to pick a side as he says it's a Scottish matter

And distanced both the Church and Rome from The
Vatican's favourite daughter

But Hillary of the US could not resist that sweet temptation

And in that wee Obama moment, she opposed the freedom
of our nation!

The Weirs and JK Rowling donated to their sides

But their generous donations have had them cruelly vilified

The Weirs received death threats and all three were abused

But the irresponsible, impartial BBC, again, discretion
used!

Then Simon Schama joined in and begged let my story be
told

But he missed our point completely, this poor man needs
consoled

"A splendid mess of a union should not be torn asunder"

But that's exactly why it should be, this union's going
under!

Information is not truths but what they think that we should
know

The more they give, the less we learn, they on us would not
bestow

The knowledge owned by just a few, who pull us to and fro

We're buried where they want us, trampled down below

Our controllers watching over us never seeing what we see

It's just as well it's down to us to vote YES to be free!

I was You.

No bed, no blanket, no TV, no home

An army of people but where are they from?

They're treated like vermin and they take what they can

Pleading for comfort, is my fellow man.

Born to be equal he lies on a street

On a shaggy old blanket, a flea bitten sheet

Unwashed and unshaved from morning to night

The world passes by, all ignoring his plight.

He's a right to be equal, a first among men

I see him each morning, again and again

His pitiful face weathered by summer's sun

His lullaby's whisky, God, what have we done?

Someone must know him, I ask him his name

His eyes look right through me then close down with shame

I'm the man who was you, a long time ago

Look into your heart, you already know.

I'm your brother, your father, yes, even your son

As you fought their battles, they'd already won

And when you've delivered they'll cast you aside

Don't worry for me, I've already died.

Fine Girls You Are.

(A wee tune for all the NHS Staff which is seriously under threat).

Fare thee well my lovely nurses

A thousand times adieu

For the Tories love of selling off

Has finally come to you

The bids came from their cronies

As did The Royal Mail's

But each and every one of them

Will escape the bloody jail.

(Chorus).

Fine girls you were

You're the girls they did adore

Their long term plan to make them rich

Worked and now you're out the door

Fine girls you were.

And now the country's raging

They can't afford their pills

For the private sector has gone mad

Up tenfold are their bills

But the secret of this wealth, you see,

Is not for us to know

It's a politicians Secret State

So their own funds now can grow.

(Chorus).

The NHS is crippled now

And soon will be no more

Nye Bevan's turning in his grave

As you're pushed out the door

The crime lords at Westminster rule

They're a cancer non-benign

I'm Alright Jack, sod the rest,

My pockets are now lined.

(Chorus).

How Pathetic!

Their campaign pamphlet's laughable, a waste of Royal mail

It's like The Sound of Music Scottish style with all its contents stale

Boys and girls laughing as they run through Highland glens

Oh! It's all a pretty picture, yes, these people are our friends!

Did someone forget to tell them, we've got brains inside our heads

It's outdated with the same old crap and each point's ripped to shreds!

They're like the poisoned dagger hidden inside a jewelled sheath

They like to show a happy face but what lurks underneath?

Miliband's just a Tory who likes to wear a Labour tag

Pandering to Tories' cuts as he holds out his doggy bag

For a share of all the profits from the sales of our assets

Better Together? This is as good as it will get!

For Scotland's part if we say NO, we'll be leading from the front

But if it's YES, he'll put up borders, he knows how to confront!

Are there borders in the EU? Are there soldiers on patrol?

Of course there aren't soldiers, he put them on the dole!

He says that we'll be foreigners and for some reason mentions aunts

Is he going to round them up, and to Scotland, them, decant?

This guy is a lunatic; the Labour party's laughing stock

Even Labour's stalwarts are fleeing from his flock

They've been the ever faithful sheep in their party's plight

But now ally with Independence, they know that YES is right!

Vote Noooooo.

Here they come, the bowler hats, wi' their bright bold
orange sash

Parading down some stranger's road as their silver cymbals
clash

The beating drums bang loudly as the flutes flow gently
passed

Their tunes are from a different age, they're the bigots
from the past.

They dress up in their crisp white shirts and wear their
shiny shoes

Oh yes, smart they are to look at, as they play their union
blues

Their tunes of God and country, their allegiance to the
Queen

To an imperialistic British Rule and a government obscene.

They're up to their knees in Fenian blood, surrender or
you'll die

 Choice words from their songbook as they play to passers-by

If you change your faith you can join them and fly silk banners high

And throw their maces upwards as they worship days gone by.

You can't ignore The Grand Orange Lodge, who I hear are backing NO

And now BT's rejected them, where is left for them to go?

It's everyone they're dead against, their statement made that clear

And when Scotland wins with a massive YES, we'll kick them out of here.

Question Everything!

Question everything you're told

Be brave, be strong, be true, be bold

Don't believe those ill informed tutors

They're bred and fed by Britain's butchers

They're meant to tell you truths not lies

And if you believe, that's our demise

For a Scotland free, look to your mind

You're our future, don't go blind

Into the room where monsters tread

And listen to their fearful dread

They're all BT, The NO Campaign

The ones who think we have no brain

YES or NO it's up to you

But vote on what you know is true

Don't listen as they bend your ear

For all they preach is biased fear.

Too Poor, Too Wee, Too Stupid!

Are we too poor to govern on our own

Are we too wee to stand alone

I thought by now you would have known

Redeem yourselves and read McCrone!

We all have dreams of hopes, desires

And to those aims we should aspire

And with Independence reach much higher

Vote NO and they'll expire.

Westminster's seed is Satan's spawn

And on their evil, we won't be drawn

They're clinging to an Empire gone

Reach for your brand new dawn.

You've milked the cow, your Northern whore

A country you sought to ignore

You're rotten to your very core

 Let The Lion Rampant roar.

I see the passion in their eyes

Proud, stout hearts are on the rise

As Saltires fly 'neath raging skies

The land we love our richest prize.

Fracking Shale.

The shared black roads that we have tarred

Will have no barbed wires, troops or guards

No sentry posts, no stringent lines

No this is yours and this is mine.

We can be great, they say we can't

As the puppets dance to the Moron's chant

The simple truths have been outlined

But though they read, fear's made them blind

They'll pay us to store nuclear waste

But the deadly toxins, our hills, will baste

Gone, will be forests, dead the trees

What's left of nature's on its knees

Now they've licenses to drill for shale

Can the earth survive, our Holy Grail,

As toxic spores seep through our hills

And by our hillsides more road-kill

Not killed by cars but dead through greed

For the shale has poisoned all their feed

Contaminants unknown to men

Run down through mountains to our glens

Destroying weeds and flowers, plants

Will wildlife die or just decant?

Can water be defined as clean

Or will its taste be now obscene?

Streams roll to rivers, flow to seas

Will sea life last or die diseased

Seventy thousand fish lie dead

From the graveyard that is our seabed

They're blaming shale, news today,

Fracking, friends, is on its way

And for what, when all is done,

 We've ample power in the sun

But the sun can't make the rich more rich

So they'll kill the earth, Ain't life a bitch!

Cameron Is A Disgrace.

Another contract duly signed but this time Parliament was
ignored

Cameron's signature keeping Trident for ten more years on
Scotland's shores

Why did he not tell anyone? Why not ask for some advice?

Is it that our men are mice or was it all about a price?

But his mate, Barrack Obama, could not help but spout

He let it slip in conference, he let the secret out.

Why did no-one know of this, was the Cabinet aware?

Of course they were, that's why they are, the not so secret
Millionaires.

As a convoy of destruction drives through Glasgow's city's
streets

Their cargo, nuclear missiles, rolling past as Glasgow
sleeps

Would you allow these on your roads with fragile bombs on
board

The after midnight sojourn journeys on but our complaints
are just ignored.

Nuclear warheads heading to the Clyde to arm Trident on
our shores

A Yes vote's Scotland's only hope, we can't take this
anymore.

No other place will have them yet they want us to live in
fear

That's no excuse, not good enough, why should we keep
them here?

Was Cameron too presumptuous, because if Scotland then votes Yes

We'll be stripping Trident to the core and its grounds we'll repossess.

A Case for Yes?

The Tories blocked exploring, our oil boom by the Clyde

Their admission only underlines we were right not to confide

They hid away McCrone's report but now after thirty years

That information's tells us, they were deserving of their smears.

As we look out to the North Sea and see rigs extracting oil

Yet behind us we see foodbanks, we don't share in the spoils

Now they're holding Euro millions back from farmers in our land

When will we see a government who are loyal to their plans?

They're scared to show their faces, they come then disappear

No questions asked from anyone, is that part of their fear?

The EU will accept us, as we're a special case

Juncker's words were turned about, that's more egg on their face

As the Commonwealth comes to Glasgow, the city of my birth

They ditched Scotland's presenters, again they showed our worth

Scotland must get off its knees and bin the scraps they feed

And stop all this embarrassment, and let the world take heed

They say this is a Union, equal on all sides

But if Westminster's the husband, we're not that blushing bride.

Contemptuous and Sleekit.

Two days before The Friendly Games, to Shetland one man came

No media, no coverage, he came to con us of our claim

The private jet had landed, our Prime Minister on board

And as he rushed to friends in waiting, the locals were ignored.

One hundred of his most elite shook each other's greedy hands

And swore an oath of secrecy, to protect their contraband

An oil rig was closed down, workers sent home on full pay

Or was it that the workers' pride had made them walk away?

They were told they must NOT say a word 'til the referendum's done

Another sleekit move from him but this game is not yet won!

Facebook's, Twitter's eagle eyes then posted up the truth

And David Cameron's Scottish view is much more than uncouth

But the YES Groups on our media sites, made us all fully aware

That the world's biggest oil field was found and we know it now as Clair.

Our contemptuous little Premier, this conniving little man

Has shown his contempt for Scotland and the true wealth of this land

They've been telling us since 97, our oil's running out

Why should we even question this, why should we even doubt

Before then Margaret Thatcher, hid 500 million pounds

Again it was from Scotland's oil, their arrogance shows no bounds

Their words were always sacrosanct or were we just naïve

But the imbalance of this Union proves, NOW IS THE TIME TO LEAVE.

The Rising Voice.

So free and mostly placid, the sea just rolls on by

With hopes against a silver moon, its easy nature lies

But if provoked, beware my friend, for a power lies beneath

And the wrath of all you ever feared, is what it will bequeath.

Relentlessly waves will come crashing down, pummeling your shore

It will retreat as though regrouping, and be stronger than before

Its voice growing ever louder, its voice is you and me

And your barricades will crumble, to the roar of liberty

Wave on wave they rise and fall, your wall is but a shield

And the ever rising power here, will never ever yield.

Jist Say Aye!

If we break the Union we'll combust

They say we could not cope, adjust

But in your back, a knife they'll thrust

Are we right then to mistrust?

Should we hold these ones so dear

The ones who've made our lands austere

The same ones who act so sincere

Who poison with their fear?

In Hades' Halls they have debates

Where cloaks and daggers evil traits

Debate on Scotland's deathly fate

Have we to sit and wait?

They say the oil's running out

We need our nuclear arms for clout

And our currency, we cannot tout

It's all lies that they spout.

On oil we've 40 years or more

It's a bonus we cannot ignore

But it's something NO should all explore

Preferably on the seabed's floor

And Trident's costs will cost us dear

If we're bombed then we'll all disappear

Then there'll be no need for their frontiers

Is it really safer here?

The pound is there for use by all

Even ministers agreed our call

And if a Scottish coinage we instal

There's half a billion costs to all.

It's your future, it's your land

Be bold enough and make your stand

Or do you want your future planned

By those who cannot understand?

Austerity.

Why can't we feed the needy, the young, the poor, the old?

Why can't we house our neighbours who sleep out in the cold?

Why is there always money to fight other people's wars

While your citizens use foodbanks cos they can't afford your stores.

For every bullet, sniper's rest, it's you who stand to gain

As we watch on in horror at the suffering and pain

But you, you see your soldiers, as your bankers on a tour

And the natives of the land you kill, they're just your guarantors.

As you pack your helicopters, your tanks and planes with bombs

To drop upon your "enemies" who would rather say salaam

And from your deadly warfare and equipment that you use

You rake in all your billions then report it all as news.

You buy the wars and train the foe and in turn they pay you

But if you live in Britain, you can join the foodbank queue

You kill abroad and kill at home, causing deaths by being austere

But with a simple vote of YES, we'll get you out of here.

Aye or Naw?

One clip of just one Scotsman went viral overnight

Were the broadcasters affronted by this most audacious sight?

They even named and shamed him, in every paper it was read

But in London when fifty thousand marched, not a single word was said!

This Sunday, two thousand more, will stand again as one

At the bias of the BBC but just like before they'll all be shunned

They don't listen to the minions for they themselves are being controlled

By a dictatorial government who leave half the news untold!

How can we give opinions when we only hear THEIR news

But it's this change that we're striving for to hear ALL points of view

Then the world's elite united, to tell every Scot what's best

With all and sundry joining in, at Mr Cameron's request

Every single one of them have made one almighty fuss

But it's a shame they'll not be voting, that one's down to us!

There's an optimistic feeling and it's racing through this land

While the pessimists put down the Scots as though we're some rebellious band

Their mirrored image reflects all THEY are with THEIR rules

As their Spin Doctors frame each quote and treat us all like fools

They've lied about their polls and oil and all our promised powers

But it's only with a YES vote, can we make this country ours.

There are vipers here in Holyrood poisoning our land

Ridiculing all our goals because THEY have nothing planned

What are THEIR aims, what goals have THEY, have THEY anything to show?

We've no guarantees, we've nothing and yet they want us to vote NO!

Scotland's Goddess.

(Chris Law, star of stage and screen (and hopefully soon, Westminster) take a bow Sir along with your team for volunteering to travel the length and breadth of Scotland in The Spirit of Independence, your converted and coveted Green Goddess).

She's not some blonde-haired beauty in a leotard and tights

But she's ravishing and beautiful and seen her share of fights

She's a model from the fifties with a rich and fiery past

Her body wasn't built for speed but it was built to last

You ladies love a fireman, pictures plastered on your wall

But the lady that they cling to, you don't see her at all

Firemen adored her and, if asked, they'd Aye say Yes

So welcome to the party, Scotland's Goddess.

She is Scotland's fire engine, Chris Law managed to obtain

For 6 weeks, a kind of mascot, our Yes Saltire Campaign

She's The Spirit of Independence, resurrected from the past

To drive our movement onwards to a victory unsurpassed

It will take a team through Scotland so wave if they pass by

Or when they stop wherever you are, come and just say Hi

They'll be touring here for six weeks and will be there just for you

And they'd love for you to come along and state your point of view

Answering your questions and they'll keep you up to pace

With all the lies that BT give, the best way, face to face,

Progressing with a promise and with a YES vote, maximise

Our chance to win our freedom, that will be Scotland's greatest prize!

We Thank You.

A sovereign nation we will be and with this liberty

We'll together build a country whose people will be free

And keep our coveted NHS with no fees for education

And the expertise borne from these stay within this nation

To ensure the wealth from oil and wind and all that we export

Stays and helps a future which assists our child support

And banish nuclear missiles with an end to poverty

And all forced unsocial justices will be banned to history

We will keep all our taxation which will stay in Holyrood

And your gratefully received donation will be used for Scotland's good.

YES Will Win.

I have seen, discussed, listened, learned and read some great debates

I've been informed, been let down, uplifted with our fates

I've seen the flags all ripped and torn and seen Saltires slashed

Stolen then set on fire with YES signs, placards smashed

I've heard of threats to property but there've been personal as well

Old men and women criticised but I'm sure there's more to tell

I've been amused and been abused, I even managed to get blocked

By several educated folk whose brains seemed kind of locked

I've seen some sites that had some sights and once was even hacked

But they never changed my viewpoint, their arguments never stacked

My conscience is convicted to the side I think is right

And I'm sure that every one of you will show them you have fight

We've the chance to rule, to govern and write a constitution of our own

We gamble with our daily lives, does separation mean alone?

There's a world of Independence that wants to share our wealth

And our NHS will thrive once more, with riches we'll bring health

To every Scottish citizen, don't let them fill you with their fear

A failing Westminster's ignored you, bring your government here

Be ruled by who you vote for and get rulings that you ask

By crossing YES on polling day, that's your simple task.

Outside is Here.

Outside in the rain, she prays for love

But a silence falls down from her Heaven above

The kids in the basement rely on their mum

But young as they are, they know nothing will come.

In our safe little houses, we like to pretend

That everything's rosy, the world's on the mend

We finish our dinner then flick on the news

And the first thing we see, is a kid with no shoes.

Our quick guilt is met with, I've nothing to hide,

As we draw our thick curtains to block the outside

You lie on the couch and pour out a beer

But your mind whispers to you, the outside is here.

Sing Our Own Song.

We're a chorus of critics, that's all, just a choir

Where we stand, what we sing, to the baton's friendly fire

They've orchestrated every word and though the chorus may be ours

It's the verses that they keep from us that hide controlling powers.

Don't let them hold the baton, refuse to sing along

Rewrite what it is in your heart, our hearts can be our song

Their verse is an agenda, handpicked by the few

Holding judgement on its content then condemn you when you're through.

Free means it's for nothing yet nothing here is free

You'll pay a lifetime over but they'll still own your liberty

Hard work counts for something but they'll always pull the strings

But if we sing our own song, we could live our lives like Kings.

If freedom's worthwhile having, lay down your demands

Stop trading online insults, you play into their hands

Focus on our positives let the union play their games

And when we run out winners, they'll have no-one else to blame.

Think about our future, of what and who we'll be

Think of our Constitution and what you'd like to see

Share with your friends and families, our new found liberty

For the song sung in September, will sing of a Scotland free.

Monsanto Kills.

(The Greed of Governments).

Pharmaceutical companies bought and you now control the seeds

You contrived to build your empire, built not from love but greed

But the greatest empire known to man is that of Mother Earth

And when Armageddon comes to us, what will your shares be worth?

Now you can poison us with medicines so we have to take some more

And the seeds you've now infected will destroy earth to its core

You are poisoning our landscapes and festering these lands

Monsanto, you must cease to be, with all your products banned!

Discoloured foods, inedible, with their insipid, bitter tastes

That's what happens to a fertile ground, all goodness is displaced

Then Monsanto's rainclouds toxic waste will float upon our skies

And the poisoned rain that falls to ground will be our earth's demise.

They've even found a loophole for the fruit and veg they grow

Forcing farmers to pay Monsanto's fee for every seed they sow

They even want to patent foods that on Europe's soil are grown

We have to stop this monster, it must be overthrown.

They're not satisfied with billions made from dusting every crop

But with the power of a signature we can force this all to stop

These people have no values or how much a life is worth

But the greatest wealth that's known to man is that of Mother Earth.

There are no cures just clients insistent on a cure

And Organic? Is there such a thing when earth itself is so impure

Their tests of toxins, cancerous, they say you are what you eat

And whilst Governments back Monsanto, they show their contempt, deceit.

The health and wealth of governments is all hypocrisy

Our planet's dying, dying fast but we're too blind to see

Mercenaries, all of them, ignoring what or who they kill

Ruled by the only thing they love, that's the US dollar bill.

We've Had Enough!

You trip the light fantastic but you're dancing in the dark

With all moves orchestrated by Jola our wee nark

That heid's a' full o' heather and it's staining her brain

And in her own country, this woman's a drain.

Her carnaptious retorts are angered lined lies

And each truth that she hears, she at once vilifies

And what of her cohort, what happened to Ruth

Has she seen the light, Scotland's Angel of Truth?

Has she said No Thanks to Better Together?

I hope that she has cos we're all sick of her

But let's get back to wee Jola, she's aye worth a laugh

She's the only one worse than Prince Phillip for gaffes

But whenever she blunders on some prime time debate

There's that mad glaikit look on a gormless face.

She never can tell when she's out on a limb

And half of her answers are made on a whim

If it wasn't for Jola and all her mistakes

I'd write far less poetry and have some more breaks

But all of those promises from our leader of Labour

Have to end now and do Scotland a favour

We're not some wee children playing in school

But they act like big kids and keep breaking the rules

You keep contradicting what you've said before

Scotland wants change and needs you no more.

As It Was, As It Is Now.

The Necropolis in Glasgow town is a place you're shown no favour

I stand alone upon its hill with St Mungo as my neighbour

If you lay here, you've lived your life and likely lived it well

And you're wakened every morning still, by the sound of Mungo's bell.

Diplomats, aristocrats, the clergy and the rich

Are all here now on equal terms, in a coffin in a ditch

Headstones so ornately carved, fluted standing high

And the self indulgent righteous, chose their words before they died.

The merchants and the moguls, shipping wares upon the Clyde

Whilst the Empire's second city, looked on as poor folk died.

Wealth costs more than riches, for money cannot buy

All the lives of ordinary folk, for a shilling, they would die.

The view they have in death could not be bought today

It's shameful then, they couldn't see that beauty in their day.

Golden laden eyelids can make a man so blind

A pound of flesh means nothing when power's in your mind.

Power, riches, wealth, are borne through exploitation

And the exploited suffered pain, remorse but always degradation.

"Rooster" David Coburn.

(A wee poem dedicated to the man from Ukip whom a lot of Scots voted for but this guy didn't even know where he lived at the time of registering)!

I hope you've satisfied yourself

With your hard thought out decision

At least you share some common traits

Like: division and derision.

When quizzed about the EU

Your champion gave it large

A stuttered silence filled our screens

Help!! Mister Farage!

Stumped at every question

This cowboy answered none

Oh! You may have picked him for a laugh

But this joker bloody won!

And at the time of registration

He gave the wrong address!

Now it looks as though he's on his way

They're a festered bloody mess!

Abortions for the unborn child,

Consumed by racist views

They're bitter, sick and twisted

From whom this bile spews.

In a country that we're trying to build

You think this should be allowed,

Your nomination sickens me, I hope today you're proud?

Heart or Mind.

When your heart and mind flow with a torturing ebb

Is it just an illusion you're caught in a web

Free up your mind and seek what is true

And share it with friends, you owe it to you

Deceit is the truth if you want it to be

Believe in their lies and they'll tell you you're free

Don't fight just accept, ignore all the fear

And if you think you're now safe then you're not really here

You're accepting the rules they've twisted before

'Til you don't know the difference and go back for more

Forget all you've learnt and see for yourself

That the truth's not in papers you stuffed on the shelf

But between every line there's a new story told

But you have to be brave and you have to be bold

And when you punch the air and you know that you've won

Your heart and your mind are now one.

My Name is Boris.

Step up, step up, I'm joining the show

I'm the mad mayor of London and want you to know

I'm heading to Uxbridge, well at least I hope so

But other than that I don't care where I go.

I miss all my pals, those Bullingdon boys

What laughter we had, such fun and the joys

We'd dress up as ladies and drown in champagne

We done what we want and will do so again

We'd be out at a party and then on a whim

Slip up to the bedroom with a her or a him

Oh we didn't care, we were young, naïve, free

All par for the course for young vibrant MPs!

In fact, we're still doing it, we don't give a toss

And we've shown Strathclyde that Croydon's the boss

We can only spend pounds if it merits its wealth

It's great news for London and cuts down on health

Ah the poor NHS, it's old, it's had its day

And my Bullingdon friends were so full of dismay

So we just had to sell it and some of our friends

Own those big private companies and I'm sure in the end

The poor folk will see that it will soon make more sense

Well, moreso to us, we'll be well recompensed.

Just think of those riches, we'll have billions to share

And then we can get back to where we once were

Bullying, partying, throwing our toys out the pram

And treating our servants like we don't give a damn

But I'll still need a space to park the old bike

So if you're up for a laugh, I'll give you a hike

And what's wrong with that, it's the life we know best

We're the elite, so sod all the rest.

The Door.

A knock on a door says you can no longer win

Do you really believe those who can't live without sin?

When the door states its morals and blows up its friends

Then tells you its wars are for peace and can't end

It'll tell you of love and will spill you its charms

As it infiltrates lands and leaves babes dead in arms

Of the mother or father who broke none of their rules

It's a conflict not war as the bombs drop on schools

And the more bombs that are dropped then the bigger the purse

As it counts up its profits, we see things getting worse

But as the door smiles at you, you can't see a face

You only hear words that no human could grace

You then look to your neighbour then look at the door

A child's family lost you can't take any more

With his whole life before him, the door killed it stone dead

Those young, happy years, replaced now with dread

But the door's poisoned mind is still sowing its seeds

With its torture and killings, its greed it must feed

And the bird that was free now quivers and shakes

And the door walks away, it doesn't make these mistakes.

Rat's Alley.

We are stuck in an alley consumed by rats

As spies hover above like black demonic bats

The sludge, the stench, the filth we feel

Like faeces stuck on dragging heels

We swipe and kick, to free, to clean

But all the while, rats run between

Siphoning what they can from us

Running deep with silent fuss

Disturbing, scheming, no respect

At best we show them dark neglect

The filth, the muck, the dirt is spread

They're prying now inside our head

They can see but we cannot

And sneak away what we forgot

We murmur moan with soft complaint

Yet with our words they twist and taint

It's treachery so watch your back

 The spies are out and out to hack

Our words are treading thinnest ice

And crawling round the trolling lice

They're after everything for greed

Controlling all is all they need

The silent screen, the soft pressed key

We're their future, you and me!

That Debate.

What extra powers will we have? Mr Darling was then
asked

But like his bed-mates could not say, is that not a simple
task?

We're working on this strategy but be sure we'll let you
know

Just two, just two, said Salmond and you'll push the vote
for NO.

But no, he couldn't tell us nor if Scotland could be rich

As an independent country; another question ditched

He would not agree with Cameron as he went on another
rant

Again, again, again he's asked but his words meant that he
can't!

Then he rattled on about currency, that our pound cannot be
shared

(But last night, his boss, Ed Milliband, defiantly declared

It would cost Hundreds of millions if we did not share the
pound

He knows if they don't accept it, they'll be run into the ground).

Darling then said the Bank of England had bailed The RBS out

Words, our friends, in the USA, would very seriously have to doubt

He's a pathological liar and for such a fervent and proud Scot

This country he says he loves so much, he hasn't shown a lot

It wasn't Salmond's greatest night but the polls had favoured YES

And although it didn't show too much, the NO camp's under stress.

Then later came the news that some entrant's had been refused

They rejected up to fifty which left the Yes camp not amused

They were beeling, having been replaced by English with no vote

So if you think the YES vote's won it, then you'd better all take note!

Another Empty Promise.

You promised us our shipyards would be safe if we vote
NO

But the lower Clyde lost its last yard, where do those
workers go?

They can't head up to bigger yards, you closed them down
as well

And still you say UKOK, this Union's Scotland's Hell.

We wouldn't need this referendum, if Britain is so great

But the fact we are, is telling you, we put more trust in our
own fate

We're aware of what's been said before and fallen for your
traps

This life is an existence as we watch our world collapse

Brick by brick it's crumbling whilst the wolves bay at the
door

If the status quo is what you want, vote NO but cry no
more.

Have you not the confidence to look for all that's right

The warning signs are there for all in big bright neon lights.

Why has there been no mention of The Clair Ridge oil find?

Why are the NO camp in denial, are they all deaf, dumb and blind

It's the biggest and the richest and it rests on Scotland's shore

It's a bonus, just a bonus, nothing less and nothing more.

But they'll have you think we're scroungers with no wealth of our own

But if we were the scroungers, they'd leave us well alone!

And did they tell you half a million jobs are geared up for the chop?

All their secrets, all their lies, when will they ever stop?

Some people are afraid of change and what they need is to believe

A belief in what this country has and have the confidence to leave

A union that is torn apart, whose obsession is with greed

Selling off our assets, an NHS our people need

It's wealth not health they think of and for Scotland have no thought

We're the northern part, too wee too poor, the land that they forgot.

Sights, Sounds and Smells.

The buildings' rust are sad remains

Like the rusted tracks from Beeching's trains

The once well tramped land is now displaced

With an iron graveyard, laid to waste.

The old stone bridge, the running stream

The factory gates where workers dreamed

The noise, the bustle, clanging steels

The blocks and tackle, cogs and wheels

The molten metal, fans of fire

The sparks, the sweat, the foundry choir.

But Alas! No more, that voice is lost

And barren landscapes show the cost

The rusted steels run slow and deep

An industry now rests in sleep

I won't forget, we can't forget

We owe our country one last debt.

Yes! I remember those halcyon days

When our engineers were never fazed

We built the biggest and the best

'Til Thatcher put that all to rest.

That Clydeside's gone and scrubs up well

But I miss its sights, its sounds and smells.

UKOK – No Thanks.

In your House of Corruption, it's for lies that you look

You're quick with the answers as you delve into your book

Do you believe all your lies to the extent that they're true?

Then you say "foodbanks are good, we all have to make do".

We know times are hard, this country's a state

And the last time you looked, was Britain still great?

You just falsify figures to suit your own needs

With zero contracts and sanctions, you enrich your own greed

Yet queues are increasing especially in deaths

It seems that you care not who gasps their last breath.

And what of your No Thanks, your followers, fans

It's not all Cybernats who bring shame on this land

In Penicuik's new Yes shop there was excrement smeared

On the brand new door handles, it's you that they cheer

Or the First Minister's death threats and the abuse which he's faced

Saltires burned and broken, stolen or defaced

And what of YES donors, especially the Weirs

Abused, even death threats while you engineered

Your portrayal of Yvonne Hama, as just the girl next door

She's a bigot, and someone, we all should abhor

It's not all one way there are scum on both sides

But at least we condemn ours while yours, you just hide.

Conviction.

A life that's worth living is richer than gold

But we see far too often our lives have been sold

They'll sell you a boat but will give you no oars

With a free zero contract to do all their chores.

This world is a circus with just too many clowns

But the public they play to have too many frowns

An English backlash is coming, we're told be aware

And the frowns they'll decay instead of repair.

They're preaching in high streets, standing on crates

Yet the crowds who they preach to don't listen, don't wait

Now Farage has warned us, we've had our lot

And tells us the English have had enough of the Scots

But we've English Yessers out knocking on doors

Whilst they draft in non-voters, like cheap little whores

They're bed and they're fed and they're driven around

And all for a pittance, they'll visit your little town.

Our voice has conviction, their words blow in the wind

We'll have the power, and their deeds, we'll rescind

The heart of this nation has a heart that is sure

And the will of its people have its future assured.

The Decider?

They took to the ring, apprehension set in

It was clear from round one who was going to win

Darling stuttered and stammered then visibly shook

As Salmond, with gloves off, threw at him the book.

Darling's body was swerving as he threw out a glance

As the victorious Salmond seized on his chance

He verbally boxed him, Darling tight on the ropes

He parried each punch and with them his hopes.

This one sided contest in our heavyweight bout

Left those undecided, at least, in no doubt

Salmond demolished the No Thanks Campaign

As the questions he asked went unanswered again!

What extra job powers can Scotland expect?

Again Darling showed why he's just a reject

Pointing his finger, as he had done all night

Wagging and shouting like a rabbit in fright

His patience had cracked, his legs just gave way

Then he mentioned the words that made everyone's day,

Darling admitted Scotland CAN use the pound

This admittance astonished and the sighs rallied round.

Then the YES voters erupted and let out a cheer

Is this finally the end of No Thanks' Project Fear?

Darling then shouted, "Don't you dare lecture me"!

I know you've 3 Plan B's but what is your Plan B?

The man was a wreck, battered and bruised

A political hiding, left hurt and abused

He'd a question avoided from a man in the crowd

If we're Better Together, why aren't we now?

One lady attacked him on our dying NHS

And blamed him quite squarely for it being a mess

I've got a YES badge, bag, flag and a band

But I can't vote at all, that's out of my hands

Now I'm praying the don't knows were watching last night

And they'll vote for a Scotland with a future that's bright.

You Change The Status Quo.

The moss has grown beneath your feet, your grass no longer grows

Your life is an acceptance and you accept the status quo

All your life they've worked on you, filling you with fear

Your eyes won't see, your tongue won't talk and your ears don't want to hear.

You hear one sided stories but every story has two sides

And until you hear both versions, how will you decide?

Are you happy with the here and now, where the poor grow ever poor

And the rich extend their riches through that secret open door

Where one NHS will be privatised and Scotland's will soon be gone

Where mass destructive weapons keep wars from us at dawn

Where sons and daughters soldier forth to fight illegal wars

Where the victors are the money men, who go home with golden bars.

Where workers go to foodbanks to subsidise their pay

Where to heat their home or heat their food is a choice they make each day

Where children starve yet money's found to arm a worthless cause

Where Lords and Ladies pass these bills to rapturous applause.

Where these so called Lords and Ladies pick up a weekly wage

For their daily spot, at The House of Lords, to sleep and cause outrage.

Where we're funding England's HS2 and London's newest sewers

So be brave enough to know yourself and take what's rightfully yours.

We are socially unequal and our society unjust

And to use your vote of Sovereignty is not only right but just

But change won't happen overnight it could be a bumpy ride

With a Yes vote we can govern ourselves with a government YOU decide.

Some say they don't like Salmond but he's not even in the race

This is all about your country, to make Scotland a better place

They can't even give a reason as to why they hate this man

The man who's given everything to make your home your land!

The Duke of Yes-shire.

Our famous Glasgow icon in spite of Englishness

Was seen charging into battle with a flag that boasted YES

Upon his head a painted cone with YES all down one side

The Iron Duke is voting YES, will he help you decide?

Now, how can you vote for someone, who thinks that he's a god?

He doesn't even live here, he nearly lives abroad

And he hardly comes to visit and it's not as if he's skint

I bet he's even got shares in, The Royal Bloody Mint!

I mean he flies up here by private jet so why stay away so long

Everything is free to him but some people think that's wrong

And all his friends they dine in style, stay in best hotels

Then claim it on expenses and no-one ever tells!

They've all got fancy houses, some have two or three

But just haud oan a minute here, does that mean you and me

Have paid for everything they've got, even down to meals

I bet we even pay their bills for shoes that need new heels!

Oh Yes, their cunning through experience, is more than just astute

They plan their treasured little wars while their citizens, destitute,

Lay in doorways, lie on streets, in makeshift nightly beds

In grotesque little corners, where their feet never tread

You've seen them yet you turn away as though they don't exist

You don't even look them in the eye as though they won't be missed

These broken men and women, who knows what's in their minds

Heartaches and the pains they feel of what they've left behind

For some it was a father, a mother or a friend

Their letters stayed inside their heads, the kind you never send

Full of their instincts, wishes and their thoughts

You'll never know the answers but you know what you've got.

Words cannot replace them, you see them in your dreams

They walk with you in silence but that's not as it seems

Words are worse than silence, words bring too much pain

They sit here in a doorway, begging in the rain

Vote Yes to change our country, let the undecided know

That the only way they'll keep us down is if you are voting No!

What Is Wrong With Independence?

Just one word, one single word, that's all it would take

But get that word wrong this once and it'll be your biggest ever mistake

It'll shut up David Cameron, now is that not worth a punt

And that halfwit Boris Johnson, is just a pure and utter ****!

Did you know that him and Farage are going for the top two jobs?

Well, they wouldn't go for normal ones, these two elitist snobs

Prime Minister OR share the post or three in one big bed

They may consider Gideon if he's not coked out his head!

But let us take them one by one, Mister Gideon Osborne

A Chancellor with a history degree, reading 80's porn

His pal was only Rothschild's son, a family super rich

And the only way he got the job was being his best pal's bitch!

And Boris-bloody-Johnson, of Croydon/Strathclyde fame

This man's so far up his own arse, he thinks this all a game

Would Boris take on Alex in a political debate

And does he think that Scotland is a northern English State?

This man who thinks that London should be a principality

A man who thinks that Scotland should shut up and go away !

Then there's Farage with his fat cigars and his bar-room brawler's stance

And a simple phrase like "Get Tae"! Tells us what Scots think his chance

A man who comes to Scotland where the streets are always lined

With Scots and other nations to show how much he is maligned

But Nigel just accepts it, takes a puff with beer in hand

And tells us what he is going to do but we don't like demands!

Are these the guys you really want, are these the ones you trust

Vote NO and that's just who you'll get and don't let them kid you on

They want Scotland's money but its people are just pawns

They've promised nothing extra, not one job creating power

What is wrong with Independence? Scotland should be ours!

Soldiers for Fortunes.

So we're going to war but who with and why

Is it for oil, more riches or just to have more soldiers die

Is it to avert our eyes from the referendum, from Scotland's prize

As you fabricate another war, it's just oil in disguise!

You know that you're not winning but you've already made some plans

You've organised a banquet with your servants all to hand

To celebrate your victory, you think you've already won

But you've forgotten Scotland, her daughters and her sons

Don't take these threats too kindly, when served with this abuse

Especially from bandits who have plenty here to lose.

They're contemptuous, disrespectful, this mob have no shame

But we can see right through them and all their snide wee games.

The NO Camp know not loyalty, they've hit a treacherous low

Disgraceful as a Government you'll now see Scotland go

We're not the ones who failed you, you're the ones who failed to serve

But we're the ones who will ensure, you get what you deserve.

Our First Minister's car was hit and pretty badly rammed

Another, and for a death threat against him, the courtroom here was jammed

Elsewhere, an egg, yes a simple egg, was crushed on Jim Murphy's back

And the media's turned on the YES Campaign and tried to paint us black

The perpetrator was caught on film and shown worldwide

But why would he wear an ear-piece? Is that what they're trying to hide?

Of the three deeds I've mentioned, "The EGG" made front page news

Well, if this is not bias, I'd love to hear your views!

If you've a land that has no worth, your rogues can live in peace

But if you're rich with oil, gas, they won't leave you in peace

Our citizens are dying from welfare cuts imposed

By our own barbaric Mafia whom The UN have exposed

Since The Freedom of Information, Westminster's been found out

Is this the time to end it all? Of that I have no doubt!

The Reverend Jim Murphy.

As the choristers gathered in the Kingdom of Fife

There preached a wee liar who feared for his life

He called it abuse but they shouted down lies

Kirkcaldy would witness Jim Murphy's demise.

But why did he do it, a speech every day?

Each day somewhere different but they all stayed away

Up on his soapbox, street perjury he'd preach

But the townsfolk so sickened, stayed out of reach.

Why would a Scotsman lie to his own

Bare faced and lying, I cannot condone

He tried for a century but had to call time

A crushed egg the culprit, that was the crime.

For disrupting events, he falsely blamed Yes

But the truth of the matter, his tour was a mess

Whoever your God is, and he gave you one wish

Would it be with Jim Murphy, listening to pish!

Some say he's demented but it's far worse than that

This Lion of Scotland has shown he's a twat

And what of the egg man, where did he go

Or where did he come from, will we ever know?

You can name us a Scotsman, in Brazil at a game

So why can't you tell us, this criminal's name?

Is he part of your make-up, is he with MI5

All part of a plan, that your corrupt mind contrived?

You pray to a country so rich yet are poor

You ally with Westminster, the blame's at your door

Your expenses will cease, you'll be run out of town

If you think London loves you, you're more of a clown!

If you have an agenda and a No vote's your choice

That's great, we'll accept that but these lies that you voice

Are NOT your opinion, you're a Westminster farce

And I hope on the 18th, you're out on your arse.

We've had this oppression for 300 years

We've witnessed and listened and will take no more fear

If a YES vote's successful, I hope there's no place

In a new Scottish Parliament, you're Scotland's disgrace.

Take with you Jola and the rest of your 'clan'

Set up your own country, create a new land

We need a new Labour, one that is true

But what Scotland does NOT need are people like you!

Your Question?

Some were against us but others were for

Some died in peacetime and others in wars

Your freedom was given, by your spirits, your god

You now walk this earth or lay under its sod.

As they laid the dirt o'er you, did you think you were free

Or was there a plot to your own liberty

Did they stop or curtail you, did they harness your strength

Did they silence you down, and if so, to what length?

Did you wish you were braver and stand up for your rights

Did you wish you could tell them to fight their own fights?

As you marched into battle in some foreign mist

Did liberty greet you, with each morning, a kiss

With today's nuclear weapons, do you think they will save

This greatest of nations or is it their grave?

Today we fight for our country and all the debates

Are all what we could be then told we're still great

What we need is courage, we need to be strong

Be brave for our children, we've been put down too long.

But how do you conquer the fear that change brings

Fear brings in with it some treacherous things

As many contrive to unite this divide

While others are saying our rights are denied.

There are many who've founded Scots pro Indy groups

These are people who canvass, our modern day troops

They battle all weathers and seek out the truths

They read between lines like an army of sleuths

Who inform their neighbours of what this will bring

And to prise off that fear to which the frightened still cling.

This country's held back, like our Unicorn chained

Now it's time to unchain us and rule once regain

We're a sovereign nation with a people that's great

Don't leave it others to determine your fate

When they lay the dirt o'er me I can rest easily

And proudly pronounce, I set myself free.

The Tea Lady.

(Who can forget this? The Better Together TV advert made this poor woman infamous).

This young lady's waited a year and a day

Now she's on the TV with her bit to say

She's holding her teacup in orgasmic stance

Today's your big day girl, this is your chance.

Do my eyes look mental, does my hair look alright

Paul's away working but will be back tonight

I mean, I need my own space but right now need my tea

There's a whole world just waiting for little old me

The Director cues Action! Oh Fuck! Am I on?

I hope I'm not squeaky and hope I don't yawn

I mean, this debate thing, what do you do?

I'm only a housewife and haven't a clue!

I mean, Paul shouts about it until he's he's bloody hoarse

But if he starts the night again, I'll file for divorce

She's fondling her cup like some sexual tool

As her eyes stop, she sidles up next to a stool

Cavorting, caressing her porcelain friend

She's not said a word and it's nearly the end

She's only a housewife who's just scraping by

And if it wasn't for teatime she'd probably die.

She's one eye on the teasmaid and one on the sink

This No voting lady has no time to think

She whispered words softly then listening, she stopped

The words from the sink said, Snap, Crackle, Pop!

Did you hear that? My friends said, I have to vote No

Well thank you dear Krispies, hoped you liked my show!

The Orange UKIP Show.

They filter through your old tin flutes to the thunder of your drums

Your maces, thrown in the air, cut through your tunes that come

From another land, another time, when bigotry was rife

We share a modern world today, why don't you get a life?

Edinburgh, our capital, is a city world renowned

But here you tarnish Scotland's streets, marching for your crown

Are you really proud of Scotland, tell me do you know

That what you'll bring to Auld Reekie's streets is The Orange UKIP show.

I suppose you've mapped out Princes Street and of course The Royal Mile

And the easy listening tunes you play, more like spewing bile

Or is it fear from deep within, are you afraid you'll lose your queen

Your King Billy took the papal purse to fight those wars obscene

The same Pope blessed both armies 'fore the fight in the battle of The Boyne

This should belong to history along with your Papal coin

Have you thought of what the locals want, as we march towards our date

A date where Scotland chooses, its own eventual fate.

With Farage booked to join your cause, it's a bigots' royal walk

The Orange Order, BNP, it's Scotland's people that you mock

The latter kicked a woman in a busy Glasgow street

Attacking pregnant women, is that some macho feat?

Westminster's rejected you, BT has said No Thanks

And if you think you'll fire up their cause, you'll just be firing blanks.

A modern Scotland's here to stay, no matter what the vote

Have you thought, on a personal note, what your tone denotes?

Yes Flags are Flying.

I value each comment, each picture, each quote

You're the ones working so hard for just one single vote

All I do is study and write on your views

They're written by me but they're all about you.

The City of Discovery way up in Dundee

Is the City of Yes, they want Scotland free

They astounded the pollsters with a near perfect score

But they pound the streets nightly still looking for more.

With a million votes missing, their work cannot cease

And the votes of their people, they're keen to increase

All over Scotland the feeling's the same

In the fight for our freedom, against Westminster's claims.

In Helensburgh, Clydebank and down in the Vale

In Orkney, in Shetland they know we can't fail

From Borders to Highlands and all in between

The Yes flags are flying, such a wonderful scene.

It's a once in a lifetime and a chance we must take

We'll forfeit our future but make no mistake

That future we'll forfeit will be more austere

They haven't denied it, they've made that quite clear.

With all that we're losing we're all bound to gain

And to accept more austerity is mental, insane

That's why they're out marching each day of their lives

They sense the injustice to Scotland is rife.

Foodbanks are rising and this country can't cope

But this referendum gives everyone hope

We'll always be neighbours and still do our trade

And to say we'll be enemies, is a game they've always played.

We'll get what we ask for, whatever we choose

And the financial experts agree we can't lose

Get rid of this Labour, the Tories, LibDems

And the Lords with their Ladies we all should condemn.

We've got nukes sit on our doorsteps and a doomed NHS

Taxes on bedrooms made to cause you duress

It's Westminster's doing, our Government opposed

But their only interest is what Tories propose!

But they didn't listen, our vote's mattered not

To vote No for this lot, can you call yourselves Scots?

You're voting for freedom but nothing's for free

And in just seventeen days, our Yes crosses will see.

A new type of country, a country to share.

Free from social injustice in a Scotland who cares.

Do Not Stop Now.

We're two points ahead in one poll but in another we're behind

But it was Murdoch who commissioned this so bear this point in mind!

Politicians perched round tables are sweating through the pain

Maybe now they realise their hopes are now in vain!

How many chances do they need? They're still up to their tricks

They're a bunch of thieving bastards, a shower of fucking pricks

Do they care about their country? They only care about themselves

What about the poor, infirm, with no food on their shelves

Those who decide between heat the house or heat up Foodbank food

We must insist a YES vote wins and rid this lot for good.

Look how they treat their citizens and what they make of wars

They gun run every country like ammunition whores

And don't care who they sell them to, they'll sell to any side

Blasting bombs to Palestine, assisting genocide

And what about the paedophiles who hide behind the law

Do you think we had forgotten them, do you think that we're that raw?

You love doing things illegal yet you say we have our rights

The very rights you want to take and the thought of this excites

The Parliament who ask for trust but who play a different game

Where every BT politician, all act the bloody same.

How can people rule like this and then ask for our respect

When they show contempt and arrogance and their people, they neglect

Now they want to love-bomb us and kid on they're so nice

Creeping underneath our skin, like a rat that crawls with lice

Be a man, be up front and grow yourself a pair

You're on a big bad borderless road and that's leading you to nowhere

The truth would likely kill you, can't you see you've been found out

And no matter what this outcome is, your Parliament's in no doubt

That the whole of Britain's on your case, your time is at an end

Oh Yes! You'll wield your power as you backstab all your friends

Just like the Brothers Milliband, one exiled, one a plum

All the friends you'll ever need? Westminster has no chums!

Where truths and powers know no bounds, where non-truths seem to reign

A lie's a lie in my book, but it seems not, in your domain.

You can't even get your pamphlets right or THAT advert on TV

And in Govan's streets, your leader led but could only talk to three

In a former Labour stronghold, they shut their Scottish doors

You've nothing here in common with a country you've ignored

Your faces spell austerity yet you think that we'll just forget

The hardships that you put folk through and don't even show regret

Complacency and apathy, we've fought them by the score

And until 10pm on polling day, we'll turn round more and more.

To a country that you want to keep, you show a deep disdain

So when you lose on judgement day, you have no right to complain

You won't be judged on future powers but what you've already done

And I don't think we'll see you again, we've had your share of fun.

Is that harsh, am I wrong, are not your policies obscene?

That's all they are, all they were, all they've ever been!

We have to keep on chapping, knock on every door

If No Thanks gain one voter, we've got to gain one more

This poll is not decisive, we've to push right to the end

An end that means so much to all, it's time to buck the trend

We can win, it's up to us, but votes are what we need

To unite and be a nation, with every colour, creed.

There will be no Utopia but at least it's our own path

And when mistakes are made by us, there'll be no Westminster wrath

But when we get it right in time, this country it will bare

A heart of social justice, where everyone will share

We know it won't easy but it's a risk we're prepared to take

Can you think of anything better? This decision's yours to make!

Off With One's Head.

(As it turns out she was pregnant!)

So little Kate, or as Scots would say, The Countess of Strathearn

Is going to bless each one of us with another Royal bairn

Please tell me when the birthday is so I can take a note

And I hope you're not just saying this, to affect the Scottish vote.

I apologise if I'm impertinent or seem a wee bit cynic

But those Westminster politicians are using every gimmick

And up the road in Balmoral, wee Cammy came to court

No! Not as the court jester; but he'd something to report

He cried: The rebellious Scots have crushed us, The Union now is dead

But the Royal voice said: If that's true, one could lose one's head

No Cammy, you're a nice young man, a relative of mine

But I will tak that cup o' kindness yet for the sake of Auld Lang Syne

But you're history you whingeing whimp, get out, get out of here

And that entity you love-bomb, fill them with more fear

My subjects in the northern 'sphere think you're nothing but an oaf

And then he bowed and then he vowed to use his bloody loaf!

As wee Cammy walked away, a brainstorm came to mind

I'll tell them I.S. are voting Yes and they'll vote No in kind

And then he thought about The Black Watch, our soldiers in Iraq

No matter what he thinks is right, he'll still get all the flak

But I was born to be a leader, he stuttered as he walked

And if there's one thing that I'm good at, it's my ability to talk

I know I sometimes veer from truths but never do I lie

I can see those Scottish faces now, if I win they will die!

Then he thought about The Warlord, the dishonourable Tony Blair

Another Scot, along with Brown, who like a good old scare

Brown can come to Edinburgh and speak of powers devolved

And I'll head back to London and don't need to get involved

Genius Cammy! Genius! You've just dealt yourself an Ace

The Scots will fall for anything and I'll keep my rightful place!

A Hundred Laboured Men.

Half their truths are blatant lies

And here they preach wi' blinkless eyes

Their jobs they cannot jeopardise

Barefaced they'll always be.

One by one they skint their knees

And left the smoke for Northern breeze

This oil of ours is no disease

Why did Labour came to town?

A hunner men came on the march

Tae quench the thirst of purses parched

And leading them their Matriarch

A Tory dressed in red.

In darkened dens they named their prize

These rich returns will be their demise

The traitors leave; their sacrifice?

The country of their birth.

We've stemmed the flow and ebbed the tide

And we, as one, now find our pride

And with controllers did not bide

We all sleep alone.

But the minds that thought there was no choice

And the roar that was a silent voice

Are now the one the ones who make the noise

They will set this Scotland free.

If we're the burden, let us go

But Westminster know that we all know

That a Scotland free can only grow

Into the country we deserve.

A sovereign people, sovereign race

Is rich enough to take its place

And the world's leaders know we'll grace

Those tables at the top.

Too Late.

They scramble with just days to go to give us extra powers

Now we lead, they're panicking, this reckless bloody shower

They reneged on their past promises so why now should we believe

When they haven't honoured these before, this time we will leave

It's illegal what they're trying to do as it contravenes the rules

It's out with the agreed 28 days, yet again they think us
fools

We're separatists and nationalists, radicals and much more

We're the scourge of Westminster as they seek to settle
scores

They signed the Edinburgh agreement, don't they read what
they sign

The high and mighty Osborne, is a Chancellor much
maligned

He's a man who's just a slimy snake looking out for
number one

And couldn't give monkeys for the damage that he's done

And his gaffer Jesus Cameron who's rushed off to meet the
queen

It's all for one and sod the rest, oh! How it could have been

But No, they wanted everything on their little silver plates

Alas! They now have nothing, the reason? They're too
late!

Belief Is All They Ask!

As Brown stood in Midlothian, he gave a speech that should enthral

He told us of the powers we'd have but mentioned none at all.

Loanhead Miners' & Welfare Club it was bile that Brown spewed

The same old empty promises, all old with nothing new

But at least he gave us dates for these, AFTER the referendum.

He over-rode wee Cammy, he of the plastic face,

A man, our supposed leader, who hates the Scottish race

At first they rejected Devo max, they didn't want it in

But that's back on the table now that Yes are going to win.

But we've heard this and more before, Scotland doesn't trust them.

But when seven hundred thousand votes are already in the post

A sixth of all the electorate are now being classed as ghosts

Cammy's coming up the road to join wee Millitant and Clegg

They're coming up to show us that they ain't too proud to beg.

For that we should applaud them, Aye! That will be bloody right

Far too little, much too late, they'd their chance to get it right.

They even flew a Saltire, well it didn't right away,

And it seemed our flag in Downing Street, just did not want to stay!

Anyway, they're coming up, and hope, to rapturous applause

But beware the smiling faces, they've come with sharpened claws!

Believe in us, give us your trust and you can have those extra powers

But why take just some with NO when YES makes Scotland ours!

The Independent Jig.

(I always think of Alex Salmond doing a wee dance for us when I read this)!

With some help from Brother Labour, it now must be believed

That Cameron destroyed this land, which no army has achieved

The Tories paid the piper but we refused to dance

They're worse than bloody useless and never took their chance.

In league with all and sundry, the trio called a truce

But their fight to save The Union was no more than self abuse

They offered extra powers that were somewhat more than vague

DEVO MAX, if we vote NO, was denounced by William Hague.

These powers that they speak of are for political campaigns

They are not a Government policy and their use must be refrained

Hague spoke today in Parliament as he took the PM's place

And spoke honestly, with dignity, this Union's a disgrace.

So now we have a timescale full of Scottish dates

But the powers devolved cannot evolve and their heads should be on plates

What a waste of Britain's public funds as they fought the BT cause

Our Government, who passed them all, don't know their bloody laws.

Maybe Alex knew this all along as he promised something big

So at Bute House, Mr Salmond please, dance your Independent jig!

Three high heid yins plus Darling with his colleague Gordon Brown

Along with Jola, Jim The Egg, it's been proven they're all clowns

Hague, he may have said it, but these bigwigs passed these bills

Now all The YES Camp have to do, is finely hone their skills.

IT'S CRISIS TIME!

You're just a northern entity, said a former Scottish son

But we'll put up borders anyway and patrol our side with guns

Labour - you have lost the plot and now your northern land,

The Yes vote now is in the lead and back in Scottish hands.

BT - you failed not only Scotland but the whole of the UK

And put all your eggs in London, UK is not OK

Cameron's failed his watch with Labour – words just cannot say

Now The PM's off to see the queen, in his northern entity.

I wonder what she'll say to him, it won't be rise Sir Dave

Oh Yes! He'll be on bended knee, beside a new dug grave

You've only days to save this Union, fail and you are doomed

I've a place for you in London's Tower, with your own wee special room.

Oh Ye Cannae Shove A Yesser Aff Their Bus.

(Just a wee daft one made up by me and Debs Brown).

Oh! Ye cannae shove us Yessers aff oor bus

Oh! Ye cannae shove us Yessers aff oor bus

If you come oan an' you're no' Indy

Ye'll be leavin' by the windae

Oh! Ye cannae shove us Yessers aff oor bus

Oh! Ye cannae shove us Yessers aff oor bus

Oh! Ye cannae shove us Yessers aff oor bus

An' when we're headin' tae the polls

Mind we won't be takin' trolls

Oh! Ye cannae shove us Yessers aff oor bus

Oh! Ye cannae shove us Yessers aff oor bus

Oh! Ye cannae shove us Yessers aff oor bus

When yer gangs are done wi' tweetin'

Ye'll be left alane an' greetin'

Oh! Ye cannae shove us Yessers aff oor bus

Oh! Ye cannae shove us Yessers aff oor bus

Oh! Ye cannae shove us Yessers aff oor bus

Ye can keep yer hoity toity breedin'

Cos we'll be singin' songs of freedom

Oh! Ye cannae shove us Yessers aff oor bus

Oh! Ye cannae shove us Yessers aff oor bus

Oh! Ye cannae shove us Yessers aff oor bus

We're the best, we're frae Dundee

And it's Scotland's YES city

Oh! Ye cannae shove us Yessers aff oor bus

Saor Alba.

No matter what the verdict be

Scotland's folk have been set free

Their minds alight, their hearts afire

They'll nae mair take the London liar.

They'll question a' and mair again

The common man will freely reign

O'er his thoughts and of his deeds

The risen Scot will now succeed.

The pain he felt now conquers fear

He cast one out and kept one near

And what he feels he now will say

Lest he be judged on Judgement Day.

And come that day will come his prayer

Look in his eyes and see his stare

The sovereign people of his land

I bow to you, my common man.

A Nation Arisen.

Let the dormant awake, rising up from their sleep

To take pride in your country, this time it's for keeps

Think not of your past as your future awaits

And know you're in control of your own country's fate.

You sit on the fence and watch them all fight

Now take up your gauntlet and do what is right.

Think through your decision and not just for yourself

For the poor who use foodbanks with no food on the shelf

For all of your brothers and your sisters as well

For the social injustice and the wars fought in hell

To rid us of Trident but still fight for what's right

To bring back a fair system that's been long put to flight

Have courage, conviction, be brave and be strong

And make your contribution, don't just tag along

Be proud and be brave but above all be true

And find that decision which represents you.

Who do you trust? Do you gain? Do you lose?

All the answers are out there, you just have to choose

This nation's awakened to decide its own fate

So empower yourself and let your voice dictate

We'll sacrifice some things and risks we will take

But we'll rise to the challenge and learn by our mistakes

Where we are going and what we all want

With no task too great, these never will daunt

The will of this nation, full of new dreams, desires

This nation's awake and their hearts are on fire.

Gordon Brown.

(Our ex PM once fought for Home Rule as chairman of the Labour Party, how times and a certain party have changed)!

He was commended by all Scotland for his lead in our Home Rule

A Labour movement chaired by him but, By God, we were fooled

His party lost their way in life as he sold off Britain's gold

Now he's fighting all he fought for as his soul was richly sold.

He undermined that gold sale when billions there was lost

Sold onto his cronies in his fire sale whilst we bore all the cost.

This Big Gun brought in by Cameron to fight on the side of No

Where their parties can't see eye to eye so

What do we do and where do we go?

Yer tea's oot Broony, we've heard a' yer charm

Who needs self abuse when you dae mair harm

Vote No ye say tae a' o' us as ye speak up on yer stage

But we read fae a different book and have mair than jist ane page.

VOTE YES.

(The Final Moments)

Will it be Yes? Will it be No?

All those questions and answers and still we don't know!

Who do you trust? Do you gain? Do you lose?

The answers are out there, you just have to choose.

The sweating, the nerves, are too much for some

But on Thursday at closing there are more nerves to come

The months of your canvassing, out with your friends

Then the panic sets in as it draws to an end

Each district, each station, each vote that's been cast

You're helpless, just watching as the long minutes pass

Slowly on slowly as the night fades away

You're hoping in hope that you managed to sway

The apathetic, undecided or ones even opposed

With the points that you made, the views you proposed.

It's all above board with not a shot fired

This country will get what the people desire.

Consider.

They choked on their words as tears filled their eyes

Appealing and begging in passionless guise

We are gutted, heartbroken yet some tears would not fall

We done all we could and gave it our all.

Beds suffered nightmares, shaking with fears,

But these fears for the future brought only more tears

Half of this country worked hard to rule on their own

They fought every minute but fought not alone

With thousands of others they had belief

That their grass it was greener; that the sun shone on Leith

But somehow Scots rejected that one final dance

When it was easier seizing that one special chance.

Some hearts were broken and so were the dreams

Independence eluded those positive teams.

Democracy won but the lies that they spread

Divided a nation but it's still far from dead.

It was thrown away but kept in reserve

Those with that dream who'll continue to serve

The needs of a people, a nation, this land

Must stay together and make a free stand.

Every leaf that you see is a flag that is flying

A St Andrew's Cross with a Red Rampant Lion

Blowing in a wind with our ghosts from the past

Shaking our hands for a moment that lasts.

Breathing the air on the paths that we breathe

In this land that we love that we all have to leave.

The beacons were lit but the fires weren't ours

They descended on Glasgow in less than twelve hours.

These were our Scotsmen, the ones who said No

The ones who brought shame to their victory show

They destroyed Glasgow's name and our country disgraced

As a worldwide audience saw our city defaced.

These violent bigots with their Nazi salutes

They don't speak for me, of that there's no dispute.

A girl on her knees clutches at her Scottish flag

But it's ripped from her grasp as her young body sags

They're burning our Saltires, torching our town

Marching and kicking folk to the ground.

It was covered by Twitter, facebook et al

But our own BBC covered nothing at all.

With Friday night revellers out for a good time

Their pathways were crossed with a regime of crime.

And what of The Vow from Westminster's three

The Vow that came through like a panicking plea

No content, no powers, just a blank page with dates

If Heaven won't help us then it's Hell that awaits.

One single agreement is NOT all that we ask

But to agree on just ONE seems an impossible task

And within twenty four hours, it seemed you had reneged

For along with your partners, on this you'll be gauged.

Cameron's mouthing to the ex mayor of New York

Swanning around, acting like some young dork

He spoke of the queen and how she likes to purr

A political blemish on a Westminster slur.

With tongue firmly in cheek he says he's suing the polls

And the ulcer he spoke of may be taking its toll.

Our minds are just prisons where we're locked up through fear

Where stopping escape are thoughts more austere

And the oil, once scarce, now will last a hundred years

Miraculously they found it all, allaying all our fears.

But for now we all go to war but will this one ever end?

That depends on what the oilmen say, the US government and friends!

Did they dream up Al quaeda and this new Islamic State?

It'll last as long as oil's found there, that's not too long to wait!

And conscription will come to your sons, from sixteen to twenty five

And there's no guarantee in war, that they'll come back alive.

And wars that we're involved in, where the mercenaries descend

Are all concocted for their money but money has no friends!

How many places do we bomb where oil does not exist?

We only bomb for riches or is there something I have missed?

Work 'til your seventy with your pension decreased

But by the time you can lift it, you could be deceased

And your winter chills will turn ice cold with your fuel assistance banned

And once fracking starts, beware my friends, you will not know your land.

Now fracking that's another tale and this is chapter one

And the instigators all have shares, we're the ones being done!

England's green and pleasant land and the valleys down in Wales

The Highlands, The Lowlands, The Lakes, The Dales

The scenic spots within this land will be drilled for gas, oil and shale

These bastards have no love of life and should all be put in jail.

Three hundred feet below the ground and underneath your house

Their horizontal drills rotate, they'll be quiet as a mouse

But they'll poison your spring waters and kill off all your feed

Not in the name of progress but in the name of greed

From John O'Groats to Lands End, there'll be six hundred chemicals spilled

To poison all our water with your fauna, flora killed.

They don't even ask permission and it's us they're meant to serve

If we say nothing to them, we get what we deserve!

And bless the good old NHS, it was safe last week they claimed

But Labour want to save it now and guess who's getting blamed?

Will England vote for Independence, I will leave that up to friends

For I will take no part in this but will watch what Twitter trends

Why shouldn't a country rule itself, stand on its own two feet

We like independence in ourselves so it's progression not a feat

And to think we would be enemies just because we self rule

Yes, they would have us all believe we're all from the same school

But we all differ as people and as such have different needs

Devolved or Independent, different colours, different creeds

A multitude of viewpoints must be considered if there's a vote

And from the 1920's I leave you with this quote:

Give me control of a nation's money supply, and I care not who makes its laws – Mayer Amschel Rothschild.

The Eye.

The Land of The Brave, The Land of The Free
Just lock up your country and give them the key
Big Brother is Watching, George Orwell was right
We've lost all that is wrong and accept they are right.

The camera's rolling, our minds are advised
To creep softly softly, and bow down to their eyes
The All Watching Eye goes wherever we go
And collects so much more than we ever will know.

The media's bribed by rich billionaires
The CIA might befriend you but for friendships don't care
It's all unofficial, though you sleep in their bed
They'll deny that they know you, your soul is now dead.

As the coins changed hands, they cleansed out your brain

And sane methods you question and now think them insane

The TV, the papers, the radio dictates

The way we should dress to the food on our plates.

You think you are free but each man has his price

They police every step with political vice

Controlled politicians, blackmailed heads of State

The puppets whose masters decide this world's fate.

They plant out insurgents in countries afar

Masterpieces of wealth, they call religious wars

A religious indictment of Lords they once praised

Their lands red with blood, their buildings now razed.

Religions and gospels, speak only of peace

But they've caused every war and wars never will cease

Are we the lambs that they mention in The Good Holy Book

Or the innocent children? Go, take a good look!

When did we last enter a war of our own?

When did we last leave oil rich countries alone?

Are religions man-made? Are all sceptics wrong?

If religions are false, what makes them so strong?

Do they belong to The Eye, The Eye that sees all

The Eye that decides who stands, who should fall

Just who are we really, do we really know

Are we the puppets in a puppeteers show?

Subject.

See as I see, seek as I seek

Speak not your mind but speak as I speak

Do all I ask and don't ask why I do

I am me. I am you.

I'm the monarch, cavalier

I am victory, the loss that you fear

I see all, I am your eyes

I am your dreams, I hear your cries

I am the one you never see

I am the ghost and you are me.

I'm your banker, soldier, spy

I'm the image of your eye

I'm the insurgent of your land

I'm the terrorist who holds your hand

I'm the one whose finger pulls

The trigger of the wealthy fools

I raise and lower interest rates

I'm the one to raise the stakes

I'll tell you when to invest

I make the rules for what is best

What to buy and how to dress

So you don't always look a mess

I tell you where to go and stay

I control your night and day

I control the world news

I give you, your points of view

I'm the medicine you need

I'm the virus that you feed

I'm the camera on your road

I'm the government you goad

I'm the chair of world banks

I'm the one you never thank

I control who controls you

And yet you tell me what to do

I decide who wins and fails

I'm the one builds the jails

I'm the one you must abhor

I'm the one who starts the war

I'm the one who sets you free

And makes you beg upon your knees

I create what you believe

I'm the one who cannot grieve

I live your imagination

I am world domination

I'm the star of your life show

But who am I? You still don't know!

The Halls of Power.

Haute coiffure and caviar

With champagne at their private bar

They tell us they're the ones we can rely on

The glory days are always here

For those who do not live in fear

At night the poor have pillows they can cry on.

They'll tax the very air you breathe

Then tell when it's time to leave

And say they're your provider

And when your time's up, time to go

They sure as hell will let you know

And feed you drugs that they call the decider.

They laugh at those who do not know

Who can't see where their stories go

For when they tell the truth, they're still lying

They manufacture deadly bugs

Then sell you their expensive drugs

Yet they always seem to live instead of dying.

And the mother of the unborn child

Who didn't live up to their style

Dies with one she couldn't love inside her

A future queen she hoped to be

Now lies in some royal cemetery

The abbey that she wed in couldn't guide her.

Their hearts are made from solid gold

From all the lies that we've been told

And laugh about some country's independence

Where they go for a top job with doubt

Then one by one they all drop out

It's not about the wages but the expenses.

They tell us how much they care

Then ask us all to pool and share

But therein lies the danger

For when history repeats itself

They find no food upon their shelves

And those who say what's best for us are strangers.

Cast Your Vote For Labour!

On the eve of this year's Hallowe'en

And although they still not have come clean

Johann took the step of standing down

Then, Anas, if I've spelt that right,

Followed suit, he's not that bright

It's the carnival and Labour are the clowns!

I thought Sarwar was a cotton thread

And the maker filled all Labour heads

With the finest, softest strands, man had ever made

They could have used pure cotton wool

But that would have made them look like fools

The Red come Blue Striped Candy Floss Brigade.

And now they reach out to us and beg

To vote for Murphy, Jim the Egg

They say he stands for us and all that's good

People see him pumping weights

Big heavy plastic Irn-Bru crates

They'll be his throne when he's king in Holyrood!

Now THE big two have both resigned

Still fed free, still wined and dined

Are destined for top jobs, wish it was me

Abroad maybe with the top brass

There's Jola kicking Sarwar's ass

While Murphy, whisking eggs he got for free!

Your Conscience.

But if souls are meant to be so free

Why put the fear of God in me?

Is it just the guilt inside my mind

Always hurtful, never kind

But whatever you have in that mind

It's not the same as mine.

Is it an alter ego deep inside

Can it be replaced, does it die?

I know it's something we can't see

But it always works against me

I know I sometimes make you mad

But you're all I've ever had

And never want to think of losing you

And believe together we can do

And what is a soul, what does it do?

And does it feel the same for you?

They say, keep your conscience clear

That's just a lonely person's fear

One day together we'll grow old

And you once you said, I've got no soul.

Murphy's Law.

He's the outlaw, the bandit, he's their hired gun

They haven't a leader, so could Jim be the one?

If the money is right, he'll put in the graft

But it's really the public he's looking to shaft!

His mind's on the money, his hand's in the till

Big Jim's going to show us the greatest of skills

If Anas' expenses were over two hundred grand

Murphy'll want twice as much in his grubby wee hands

But this Scottish Houdini can make cash disappear

Then Hey Presto! In his own account, the cash reappears!

He's a soldier of fortune of no real distinction

And knows Labour is done for and facing extinction

He's in for the money as all mercenaries are

He's in it for power but they think he's a star!

Well, who'd want a job when their party's going bust?

A man they call Murphy, the man we distrust.

How much will he make between now and next May?

He wouldn't be going for it to end up dismayed

He knows what he's doing, he's going in for the kill

The last heist he'll pull, this man of goodwill.

Their flag that once so proudly flew against the bluest sky

The richest red, we gazed upon, flying free and high

But that now seems so long ago, the rallies on the Clyde

Have long gone, and that party, in so many hearts have died.

The flag we raised so long ago is unfurled at half mast

A relic in our memories, from the workers of the past

The working class does not exist in the world of today

No union leaders standing up for what we have to say

They're careerists for a single cause with inner fighting rife

Full of flaws, divided, bringing bitterness and strife.

They're leaving in droves, they know it's the end

Like Caesar and Brutus, who are their friends?

If Murphy takes that vacant seat, beware of the attack

The long red knives are waiting, for Alexander's back,

It seems Murphy hates anyone who gets in his way

The power and riches, the only reason he stays.

What Colour Labour?

As red Labour bed blue Tories, a threesome springs to mind

So colourful this Labour lot, now with Orangemen they've aligned

They came from Norn Irn as loyal subjects to the King

But to them, the land they came to, meant not a bloody thing

There's a rainbow over Scotland but the colours are a mess

It feels like the Nazi party with its leader Rudolf Hess.

A scandal throughout Scotland but it's not reported in the news

It's Scotland's news for common Scots but they heed not Scottish views

They say they're backing Labour to hold onto their seats

With thousands joining the SNP, will they be able to compete?

Their members are not happy and say their leaders are to blame

Let them bed the Orangemen but not in Scotland's name

Miliband and Lamont, two fools who've lost the plot

Have betrayed the Labour Party that was founded by a Scot.

Red, Yellow and Blue.

The police were there at YOUR command

And now they want eight hundred grand

You defaulted but we'll take cash in hand

Or see you soon in court.

Will they pay up or go to jail

For this amount they'll skip bail

Is Holyrood their Holy Grail

They're all experts at playing parts of Judas.

Did Jesus come then go away

No trusting words they had to say

Can Ruth and Willie find a way

Of fiddling expenses just to pay it?

They put them on the bad debts list

The list they thought did not exist

But now they've felt the Judas kiss

They're coming.

These Reds and Yellows don't align

They can't even draw the Party Line

To us they play deaf, dumb and blind

But the hangman's waiting just around the corner.

The ones in red have paid their debt

They haven't got a leader yet

The Devil's playing hard to get

So they're waiting on another favoured sinner.

Brown's bowed out, he knows the score

Gold doesn't pour from every pore

His back is bent, his fingers sore

Just another Judas counting all his silver.

Left or right, where do they stand?

The Devil's dealt them their last hand

And won't allow what they had planned

Soon they'll be gone, gone and gone forever.

The Lullaby of The Clyde.

The faint purple hills fade with sunset

The cue for the kids' lullabies

Explosions of pinks cover Glasgow

As it devours the earlier skies.

Another daylight bows out over Glasgow

To bring on its beautiful show

And the darkened wall from the old gable end

Lights up as if calling on friends,

The whole city's awash with its glory

Spreading as though it's on fire

Brushed crimson shines and the bold skyline flames

Illuminate Glasgow's old spires.

But the pearl of them all is our river

Our jewel of the Glaswegian crown

Winding and twisting this silk ribbon shines

As it travels, gently up and then down.

Like a silk silver ribbon it twists in the night

Rolling o'er boulder and stone

Floating by lovers behind bright city lights

To some it's all they've ever known.

The shimmering ribbon flows forward

As the children in bed miss its song

Past spaces where there used to be shipyards

The Empire's hub for so long.

I see men in their thousands, the ghosts of these yards

Flat capped and brimming with pride

For one special moment they wish they could be

Building again on The Clyde.

As I look on the river and what I see now,

There's hardly a boat to be seen

Empty quays sit by new houses built

Where the boats and ships would have been

But I comfort myself with the knowledge

That I saw those halcyon days

When Glasgow had magical powers

And the world bowed down in its praise.

They went neither to Europe nor to the Far East,

Clyde Built was the name they all knew

It was trusted, renowned, built here to last

We showed them what we could do

But this may be our farewell, our last ever adieu

And loneliness will fall when it's gone

But tonight and for always this river will flow

And will again, wake our children at dawn.

Why?

Are the fires still burning, are the skies still alight

Are the ghosts of the dead still looking to fight?

Were the bayonets still shining or were they covered in blood

As you peered out of your trench to a field washed with mud.

Can you still hear the bombs as they pass overhead?

Did you think yourself lucky as your comrades lay dead

But a million more soldiers will go there again

Did you really think wars were intended to end?

The bombs, mortars, bullets from both sides they poured

But to fight for this peace, we are weapons of war

In some barren desert, in some killing zone

They fight and they fight until everyone's gone.

 What did they die for and how many must die

I know they won't answer but I'm still asking why

When they gave you a tag with a number, no name

Did you not realise then you were part of their game?

Royal medals hang proudly yet they've not fired a gun

While our soldiers like dominoes fall one by one

In a field of their choosing at a time of their choice

They command you to kill in their right royal voice!

Did you write me that letter, did you sing our song

I wish you were here, here is where you belong

But that road where we parted was so different back then

Someday we'll be together but they will say when.

Nicola Sturgeon, First Minister of Scotland.

(The Queen of Caledonia).

On a cold and damp Perth afternoon, with emotions running high

The people's man, bade a fond farewell, and said his last goodbye

A tear or two appeared in eyes as our first lady took the stage

And then a few more tears were shed, as she kissed her outgoing sage.

The master had his reasons and thought it time that he stepped down

And now, the Queen of Caledonia, would accept the people's crown.

We knew she was formidable as she has proven in the past

These were different expectations but did this lady have the class?

She caressed the stage with tartan shoes to match her tartan heart

And with a smile of acceptance, acknowledged her new part

It's a monumental task ahead but she's capable for them

She's had the best of teachers and now she's at the helm.

She'll fight for all he stood for and demand her views are heard

For even now, adversaries, are afraid and running scared

They're afraid because she's capable but they don't know to what extent

They'll find out just soon enough and they'll find out what she meant.

By what it means for liars and why they can't, must not, exist

Then she gave to us her promises and sealed them with a kiss.

To tell a lie to anyone, you first must know the truth

But to attack the poor, the needy, they are no more than uncouth.

And to all those who have divided, she gave promise to unite

And to all of you who stood back and watched, you should all now stand and fight

The people here have chosen you as champion for their cause

And the mantle some thought too great, now rests firmly in your claws.

I won't embellish on your words, nor of the stage you made your own

And although it seemed a solo act, you were never there alone

As Scotland's new First Minister you'll take a nation and ascend

To the heights, deserving of a people, and whose alliance, they extend.

The City of Yes.

In the city of Yes, sometimes known as Dundee

There are artists, musicians where everything's free

If you've something to say, they'll lend you an ear

But they'll take it right back if they don't like what they hear.

But the folks of this city are warm with minds free

And a welcome awaits you - that might not include me

But I've so many friends there, some of whom I've never seen

And they all voted Yes: Oh! What might have been!

They all read The White Paper then The Common Weal

And right up to voting thought a victory real

They've even Yes transport and one that's driven by our Chris

But were let down by, what's known as, A Scots' Judas Kiss.

But instead of just dying they continued to rise

And called on all Scotland to open their eyes

Oh! Yes, they were gutted, they were all in a mess

But Dundonians showed Scotland that their vote was Yes!

Most Scottish voters didn't see it that way

And put an "X" in the No box on that fateful day

The Discovery was built here and left them its name

And they discovered that losing needn't bring on any shame

But if it were now, I'm sure they'd succeed

They were beaten by lies all borne out of greed.

They fought so that hardships here, could be redressed

And chose hope over fear in The City of Yes!

Great Britain 2014.

For positions of power, they're constantly vying

Then look on as parents and children are dying

Mentally, physically, they're crippling inside

And each day that passes, brings more suicides

Yet our leaders have meetings to help these poor souls

But their answer to poverty is to cut down their dole!

Some families working don't fare any better

Dreading their days and hiding from letters

The bills, the court warnings, stating they're in arrears

They're living a nightmare and know only fear

No food on the table and none on the shelf

He's found in the attic, he's just hung himself!

A mother out shopping leaves her newborn behind

She knows it is wrong but thinks she's being kind

What chance have her children if she can't give them food

But soon she's arrested and locked up for good

She was only a mother doing what she thought best

An inmate then kills her, so who failed the test?

Our government just go on and sanction the needy

While the fat cats just go on, getting more greedy

They'll just have a banquet at some fancy hotel

While the poor, they're discussing, are halfway to hell

If God has an answer and if God is all good

We need a God who can play Robin Hood?

The powers that be want a medal for valour

While the poverty stricken are living in squalor

A mother's now working down some city backstreet

Selling her love to some stranger she meets

But back home wrapped in blankets is a lonely young child

They've to wait until morning 'til they're reconciled!

This is our Britain, the one we call Great

Where our workers can't put food upon their kids' plates

They fear every moment but onward they strive

How long will it be before we lose more lives?

But nothing's addressed, with no real reviews

And nothing's reported in the state controlled news!

One in five Scots live below poverty's line

Yet Westminster will tell you that everything's fine

A friend of mine stated he'd no answers to questions

Posed by the blighted as they lose their possessions

Put out on the streets through a mortgage unpaid

Another life in the balance as they don't make the grade.

Trolls.

With warring type names you could never forget

They're meant to be friends but we've never met

They sift through your pages and follow each post

Like celestial beings, they float round like ghosts

I don't know them from Adam but they seem to know me

They'll pounce on you when you are wrong but hide when you are right

The laptop loonies speak their piece but they talk utter shite!

These modern day warriors will fight day and night

But put BOO! In block capitals and they'll all die of fright

Their sword and their shield is a wee board with keys

And they give themselves honours in varying degrees

Their ridiculous manner is beyond ridicule

And sometimes I wonder if they ever saw school

These poor hapless people talk nothing but crap

And most normal people want to give them a slap

These hardmen of tech, down the keyboard they scroll

Welcome to Facebook and welcome to trolls!

A Political Diamond.

Some achieve greatness while greats go on achieving

Some will never leave you, even though they say they're leaving

Some become a legend, some become a myth

Not just, for what they done, but what they leave you with.

Some will ask for nothing asking only for respect

Some ignore the mighty yet to the poor show no neglect

Some will stand behind you leaving you to take the reins

Applauding in the shadows, so proud of all your gains.

Some accept the adulation but to others gives the praise

Being strong in tough times, greats don't show they're fazed

Bullying when need be but stands up to the same

He beats the men who made the rules in their silly little games.

He's gone and going nowhere now but this man's coming back

He'll be rolling like a steam train along a different track

Look out for this man Westminster; look out for this wee diamond

He's a cut above the rest of you and his name is Alex Salmond.

How High Should We Jump?

Darling Lamont Brown, this is isn't just one person but three of a kind

But before they could face their jurors, they jumped ship and resigned

It was never for the power and certainly not the treasures

Brown tells us it's an honour, and for him, the proudest pleasure

To serve his friends and neighbours and what it all has meant

To a man who never felt the pain of his constituents!

They realised he was lying but his "charm" pulled him through

Yet still he lied and still he charmed 'til they saw his points of view,

This dirty rotten scoundrel found his starring role

In Scotland's referendum, where he sold his Scottish soul.

He said every Scot had legal rights stay with Team GB

He even under-wrote the Vow, and we don't know what that'll be

And Cameron's under pressure, to uphold that promise made

But Brown was the assassin, the trap was his, he laid.

And what a speech, a sucker punch, when we thought he'd stay down

But No! He sucked in more than half, our ex-premier, Gordon Brown

Now he's stepping down for good, his plan was scripted well

And we won't have that satisfaction, of sending him to Hell.

We can't humiliate him, or Darling, his "best friend"

These two had argued tooth and nail right to the very end

Yet stayed long enough together to hear all their Westminster's friends

Spin their tales of doom and gloom, yes, they both sold out this land

But there were others, namely Jola, it was every day she lied

Then resigned, and blamed wee Miliband, saying Scotland's hands were tied!

That was *after* No gained victory, why not say something *before*

She's just another Labour traitor, gutless to the core!

Brown was the protagonist and back then he was criticised

But now he knows the truth of it, he knows now he's despised.

The National.

"The National" paper hit Scots' streets today

Yet more than a million were left in dismay

Stockists were few, and said, some larger stores

You lot are the type we all should ignore!

A paper for us and it's pro-Independence

Not stocking it equals they've no business sense

THEY are fighting a battle that's already done

But the war carries on and still to be won.

We have freedom of speech and we've freedom of choice

We'll vote with our wallets, not with our voice

They think they know but they haven't a clue

Why are sales down? That's all down to you!

You were smug when you sided with Better Together

But now we could knock you all down with a feather

No profits to speak of, who's now in charge?

The only cruise you'll get is one on a barge!

You laughed when we told you an embargo was due

On Tesco with others and Sainsbury's too

Oh Morrisons, don't think you are escaping the wrath

The public have spoken and have the last laugh.

Aldi and Lidl, they supported our cause

Flying the Saltire and breaking no laws

Their profits are up and still on the rise

They're rubbing their hands, not drying their eyes!

Is "he" the End Of Labour?

This man will go to any length to get his name in print

The man we know as Murphy who has nothing more than stints

That drone, that ever dulcet tone, has told us he's distressed

And today he asks for all our help to aid him on his quest.

This sojourn of redemption is to right the wrongs he's done.

A noble cause? You decide, he's a man who's on the run

The people who are hunting him, are the people he betrayed

This minstrel's had his swan song, on this final masquerade.

He wants to fight austerity with our FM by his side

A squirming move to wriggle back and save his lying hide

I'm sure he thinks our First Minister will swoon at this request,

A reformed man? In just two months? I think the man's possessed!

He'll always be Jim The Egg, who spoke from plastic crates

The man who spoke to dozens with a voice that always grates

He wants to help the poor, the old, which is such a noble cause

But he's one of those who caused their ills and now seeks our applause!

Do Labour voters trust him? Not from what I hear or see,

They're leaving in their droves to join, The Greens and SSP

But the SNP has risen most with our FM now on tour

And with this lady's leadership, our country will mature.

DEVO MAX - Westminster Style.

We got what Scotland asked for but it falls short of what we
need
This nation of divisive plans drawn up by different breeds
We now have no neutrals in this land, none sit upon a fence
Only those who take the time to think and those who think
they've sense.

Even Parliament's divided on the powers we received
They it was disgraceful whilst Labour were relieved
So that's your lot, the PM said, in fact I'm rather pleased
Well, that's the Scots all happy now, they're easily
appeased.

Think again son, think again, The Wide Awake Club's here
You frightened most into voting No so let me make this
clear
Do you really think this is enough, we rejected more than
this
You've taken all we ever had and now you take the piss.

Sweeping powers said the news but we all know they're
your words

We're daft but we're not stupid, you think us Scots absurd!
We thought this would be Devo Max but it's still
Westminster rule
You failed us all dear David, we're not your Eton fools!

You have no sense of justice, no heart or conscience, soul
And the other two that make your three are not fit for the
dole
How can you say you're Christians when you let your
people die
Of starvation, malnutrition, the lives you live are lies!

You talk about economy and rave about its growth
You took a vow to serve us all and swore upon that oath
You are meant to serve us and by us, I mean us all
But you hold the rich above your head and watch the poor
man fall.

The wrath of Scotland beckons, it's no more The 45
The No votes wakened up to you, Scotland is alive
Look at how our parties rise whilst you're in disarray
The undertaker's standing by, Scots will have their say.

The Unicorn.

Last night I saw a Unicorn, so wild, running free

And through the wooded forest, ran, passing every tree

Then slowly stopped and rose so high, his wild hoofs
kicked the air

And I watched him toss his great white mane; he knew not I
was there

For man may never touch him, touch not hair nor hide

And he wears no more, the golden chains; they lie now by
his side.

The End? That's up to you!

Index.

263

Thank YOU.

I am very grateful to those who asked me to put all my Indy poems into a book and would like to say a big thank you to all those concerned. I can't remember all the names so if I have missed you out, please accept my apologies. I thank Lorraine Shaw & Alan Canon (more Glasgow than Glasgow itself), Pat Brusnahan & Eric Northcote for all their input, Dawn Hitchings & Amy Wood (who were the first people I looked to for advice), Julie Macgregor (whose Scottish songs inspire), Jackie Pettigrew Morrison, George Boland, Reid Morrison, Debbie Gallagher (who is going to write a book about growing up in the 80s), Karen Brownlee, Chris Law & Jacobyte MacLachlainn (thank you for getting them out there and get well soon), Helen Hemphill, Sheena Kershaw, Dippy Lala, Carol Reid-Taylor, Catherine Clark-Holman, Sir Gordon Spence, Lilly Gallagher, Amy McKechnie, May Hooper, Sheena Lumsden, Sadie McCallum, Janice Sinclair, Evelyn R Airlie, Yvonne Smith, Karen Gillies, Jonny Plywood-Burger, Anne Reid (thanks for reminiscing about Scotland and glad you're up and about soon), Sandie Forsyth, Indy Deb, Stephen McDonald, Elizabeth Glen Bowers, Heather McLean, Michael Duffy, John McLaughlan, Eddie Smith, Isabel Cowan, Pamela Lemon, Rupert Weir, Alan Weir, Liz Cairney, Norma Johnson, Rhonda Cooper, Wendy Shaw, Marion Plunkett, Pat Plunkett, Janis Christine MacKinnon, Fiona Mclaney, Kenny Robertson, Karen Jamieson, Indy Yvie, Shirley Grant, Clare Tereasa Gallagher, Kenny MacKinnon, Fiona Stewart, Pat Lee (for reading them in public and putting them on YouTube), Jemma

McLaughlan, Sarah Barwood, Fiona Wallace, Alex Glasgow Airlie, Michael Skribbles, Andrina Morrison, Shuggie White, Garry Cross, Lily Zotou, Sharon Ereza Ferrie, Christine Kabashi, Frankie Jack, Kelly MacDonald, Terry Walls, Jessie Pettigrew, Rosemary Forsyth, Cathie Bernadette Coll, Caroline Drinan, Sean Cahill, Gill Williams, Sandra Nel, Amanda Brown, Dot Russell, Jordi McArthur, Sion Rees Williams, Jean McClung, Sharon Wynne Mcintosh, Stephen McGinty, Remi Joanne Morrison, Heather Turner, Fiona Carmichael-Tweedlie, Karen Gillies, Elaine Milmine, GaelForce Crafts, Ada Cartwright, Debs McDonald, Sarah Hempy Jane, Daneli Mayoh, Maire nic Criosta, Josephine Caird, Sarah Dudley, Evelyn McCulloch, Isobelle Shaw, Geordie Farmer, Alan Mcphail, Bob Costello, Janice Dewdney, Mick McMenemy, Wendy Shaw, Terence Christie, Adela Johnstone, Fred McNeill and last but certainly not least, Alison Rollo. There are so many more so please forgive me if I have missed you out.

Thank you all for your encouragement and for making this book possible. Paul x

Saor Alba.

Made in the USA
Columbia, SC
29 August 2017